# HOT SHOTS

**FLAMING
DRINKS
FOR DARING
DRINKERS**

CIDER MILL
PRESS

BOOK
PUBLISHERS

Kennebunkport, Maine

13-Digit ISBN: 978-1-60433-185-1
10-Digit ISBN: 1-60433-185-2

This book may be ordered by mail from the publisher. Please include $2.95 for postage and handling. Please support your local bookseller first!

Books published by Applesauce Press and Cider Mill Press Book Publishers are available at special discounts for bulk purchases in the United States by corporations, institutions, and other organizations. For more information, please contact the publisher.

Cider Mill Press Book Publishers
"Where good books are ready for press"
12 Port Farm Road
Kennebunkport, Maine 04046

Visit us on the Web!
www.cidermillpress.com

Design by Melissa Gerber
Typography: Dirty Seven Two, Din Condensed
Printed in China

1 2 3 4 5 6 7 8 9 0

First Edition

# DEDICATION

We dedicate this book to all the master mixologists out there.

# DISCLAIMER

Dude, you're playing with fire here. Sooo, take all of the safety precautions in this book way seriously. Lighting alcoholic drinks on fire without considering safety is stupid. Drinking shots that are still on fire is even stupider and should NEVER be attempted. You will get messed up bad. And you may also end up burning up lots of s#*t like your bar, your house, your friends ... you get our drift. Also, if you screw up and light your face on fire or burn down every home on your block, it's not our fault. If you try to blame us, we'll just say, "We told you so." We will turn our backs on you and deny your existence. And footage of your idiocy will most likely make its way onto YouTube.

# CONTENTS

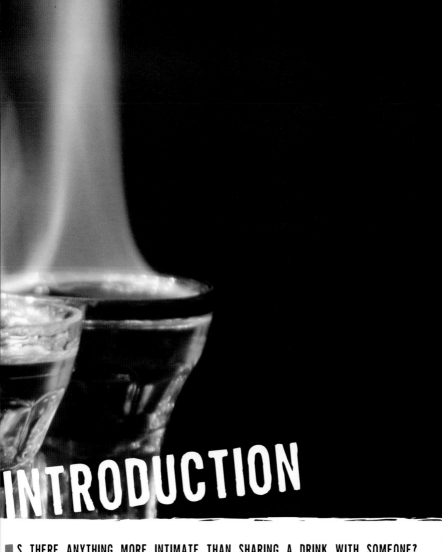

# INTRODUCTION

I S THERE ANYTHING MORE INTIMATE THAN SHARING A DRINK WITH SOMEONE? PERHAPS BREAKING BREAD OR DOING THE HIBBIDY-DIBBIDY . . . BUT OTHER THAN THAT, FEW OTHER THINGS.

If you want to put an exclamation point on your time with your friends and loved ones, whether in an intimate setting or at a festive party, consider the unique addition of a flame to your libations of choice. When executed carefully and thoughtfully, a flaming drink is a great way to get everyone in the mood for a fun evening or to put a capstone on a decadent meal. There's something thrilling, even mesmerizing, about the brilliant blue flame that arises from setting alcohol alight. Maybe the excitement comes from that naughty feeling of doing something dangerous; after all, your mother always told you not to play with fire. Well, the DANGER factor of this act cannot be underestimated (please, please, please read Fire Safety Tips on page 16 prior to making any of these drinks!). But when done in a carefully controlled environment, a flaming drink can serve as a cool visual highlight of whatever event you're hosting.

In this book you'll find flaming drink recipes to satisfy a wide range of tastes, styles, occasions, and, of course, bartending prowess. In fact, *Hot Shots* could serve as a lifelong companion. As your tastes and needs grow beyond keggers on the rooftop and tropical drinks on the beach, simply continue advancing through the chapters, where you'll find plenty of drinks to suit the new social demands of your life, whether that's charming a date, entertaining clients, or hosting an annual holiday party. The icons that come with each recipe will help you choose the right hot shot for the occasion; see page 28 to decode them.

The first two chapters of recipes are mainly shooters that are relatively high proof and easy to construct. With the majority of these drinks, the flame is merely part of the show you're putting on for your guests to prove your manhood (or womanhood), make a memorable party, get some hottie's attention, or whatever other bombastic reason is driving you to light alcohol on fire.

The remaining chapters feature more sophisticated drinks including hot coffees, grogs, glöggs, old-school flaming punches, and a handful of exciting contributions from great bars and restaurants around the world. Making these drinks will have you flambéing; flaming zests; igniting brandy-filled ladles; and toasting coffee beans, cloves, and spices in a brandy balloon. Some of the techniques presented in these chapters are quite advanced. We heartily recommend that you read the instructions carefully, practice before you attempt to serve more elaborate (i.e. dangerous) flaming drinks at a party, remember your fire safety essentials, and when in doubt, leave it to the professionals. After all, there's a reason people go to bartending school! If you did not, sometimes it's best to step aside and let the maestros do their thing.

In fact, the art of the cocktail is making a comeback around the world. It's becoming easier and easier to find a local haunt that has a creative cocktail list and talented bartenders who have genuine respect for the cocktail's rich history. (This includes the talented mixologists who have supplied the fabulous "Out on the Town" recipes scattered throughout this book.) Seek them out if you want to watch citrus oil ignited to create a flaming zest, a sugar cube flambéed with brandy, or flaming alcohol poured back and forth between cups to create that showboat of the golden age of cocktails, the Blue Blazer. You'll enjoy the spectacle, and it may inspire you to make your own daring drinks!

# BEFORE YOU LIGHT THINGS UP

Like any savvy host or hostess, you wouldn't attempt a lobster Newburg or a chocolate soufflé for the first time with a house full of guests milling around. If you choose to give your party or gathering the verve provided by flaming drinks, you'll want to have the right tools on hand, appropriate drink choices for the occasion, all your safety considerations taken care of, and enough practice under your belt so you don't make a flaming idiot of yourself in front of your guests. So, read this section carefully before making any of the recipes in this book. We'll keep it short and sweet for you antsy folks!

# YOUR CANVAS

The first thing you need to figure out is where you're going to make and light your drinks. Choose a clean, dry counter, bar, or table to use as your staging area. Keep it clear of rags, alcohol spills, and any tchotchkes that could accidentally catch on fire when you light your shots. Look above your head: Is there anything dangling (be it party decorations, curtains, or a lampshade) that could go up in flames? If so, remove it. Look at yourself: Are you wearing loose long sleeves or loose long hair that could catch fire? Bangles that could knock something over? Roller skates? Choose a new look for the night.

You should also remove any bottles of alcohol that are not part of the recipe you are preparing, and replace the caps or corks on alcohol you are using as soon as you finish pouring. Worst-case scenario: Someone knocks a bottle of booze over while you're lighting a match. You get the scary picture.

Before you prepare flaming drinks, always dim the lights. Flames from alcohol are almost invisible when you're in a brightly lit room. You want everyone to be able to enjoy the show! (And you also want to be able to see that the flames are extinguished afterward.)

# TOOLS OF THE TRADE

You don't need a ton of fancy equipment to create most of the flaming shots in this book: just some shot glasses (these range from 1 to 2 ounces), a match or lighter, and did we mention the all-important fire extinguisher? Get one.

## GLASSWARE

Once you've mastered the art of the hot shot, you may want to move on to some other stylish techniques and pick your glassware accordingly. See Bartending Tricks & Techniques (page 21) for descriptions of the techniques used in this book.

Each recipe in this book includes an icon indicating the recommended glassware for that drink (see page 28). That isn't to say you *can't* serve a Flaming Hot Chocolate in a beer stein; just be prepared for your date's reaction to match your level of effort.

Important: Only use heatproof glassware. If you add a blazing-hot gallon of punch to a bowl that's not heatproof, the bowl could crack into bits, and you'll have a big old flaming inferno on your hands. Seriously. We aren't kidding. It will happen if you're not smart about this.

# MEASURING INSTRUMENTS

To keep things simple, whenever possible, we've supplied ingredients in ratios (see Mixing and Measuring on page 18 for more on this). But some of the fancier drinks and punches that contain a longer list of ingredients actually require you to measure the amounts of alcohol going into the drinks. For that you'll need some jiggers, which are stainless steel cones that provide back-to-back measures for 2-ounces/1-ounce, 1 ½-ounces/¾-ounce, and 1-once/½-ounce. Jiggers are super useful and, happily, super cheap.

You'll also want to nab some measuring spoons from your kitchen: 1 tablespoon (1 ounce), ½ tablespoon (¼ ounce), 1 teaspoon (⅙ ounce), and ½ teaspoon (¹⁄₁₂ ounce).

# LIGHTING EQUIPMENT

A campfire lighter or long match will do the job and keep things casual. But if you're an artiste, consider eschewing the use of a butane lighter or sulfur-spewing matches to avoid compromising the taste of your carefully constructed libations. Using bamboo skewers or even chopsticks (which are often made of bamboo) will help you avoid infecting your drinks with unwanted flavors when you light them. These will also allow you to keep your distance from a big ol' flaming chafing dish or punch bowl.

# THE BOOZE YOU'LL USE

Many of the drink recipes in this book call for several different boozes and liqueurs, and you'll always need a flaming agent (overproof rum or something else that's easy to ignite). So, unless you're a flight attendant with unlimited access to minibars, don't feel like you have to stock up on every booze mentioned in this book. Just pick the flaming drink you want to make, then consider that your shopping list as you head out to the liquor store.

One essential item you *can* keep on hand is your flaming agent. Most of the drinks in this book call for overproof rum. Why? The alcohol level is really high (151 proof, or more than 75% alcohol), which makes it super easy to ignite. (In fact, sometimes too easy: See Fire Safety Tips on page 16.) A few of the hot shots call for Everclear (another 151-proof booze), but alas, Everclear is only legal in some U.S. states and Canadian provinces, so as with sodomy, you may need to take a little road trip to indulge with the Law's blessing.

To be ignited, the flaming agent must be at least 80 proof (40% alcohol). But even then, it can be difficult to get the alcohol to light. Don't be tempted to simply splash more alcohol in there or you may *really* get a fire started. Instead, when a recipe uses an 80-proof spirit such as brandy or whiskey as the flaming agent, we often suggest that you warm the alcohol a bit since raising its temperature will make it easier to ignite it. To do this, simply rinse out the glass with hot (or in some cases even boiling) water, then add the alcohol to the glass.

# FIRE SAFETY TIPS FROM OUR FRIENDLY NEIGHBORHOOD FIREFIGHTERS

For those of you interested in throwing a lovely party with the fun addition of a flaming cocktail, the following are some words of advice from two of New York City's Bravest: Chief Mike Casey of Ladder 1, who also happens to own the bar, Red Sky, and Kevin Wrafter, an eleven-year veteran of Engine 6. When preparing and serving flaming drinks, they urge you to:

- Be cautious.
- Do it in a controlled environment.
- Keep a fire extinguisher on hand. (It needs to be capable of putting out the type of fire you have started. Type ABC extinguishers can put out fires involving combustible or flammable liquids, including alcohol.)
- Do not place open bottles of booze near a flame and never pour alcohol from a bottle directly into a flaming dish or punch bowl. (The flames may blow back.)
- Dim the lights so you can see the flames (and make sure the drinks are completely extinguished before drinking).
- Don't invite dopey people to your party.
- Don't be a jerk.
- Use long matches or skewers to light your drinks (see page 15).
- Don't be a moron and attempt to drink while your drink's still flaming. Don't suck it through a straw either. (If you need convincing, check out the many videos of fire-breathing partiers posted on YouTube.com.)
- If the drink is in a glass, put out the flames with an empty glass or blow them out. If you have a punch bowl of blazing booze, put a lid on it. If you have a burning spoon or ladle full of alcohol, dip it into your drink and stir rapidly. (Just remember, if your drink contains additional alcohol, that may catch on fire too before you put out the flames.)
- Never drink flaming drinks drunk.
- It's one thing to **be** the life of a party, but don't **end** a life at a party!

See also Fire Safety—What NOT to Do! (page 17).

# BEST WAYS TO EXTINGUISH AN ALCOHOL-RELATED FIRE

* Smother the flames with a wet towel.
* Use a fire extinguisher (Type ABC, as discussed on the previous page. Keep it nearby or it will do you no good).
* Stop, drop, and roll if *you* are on fire.
* If you cannot put out the fire quickly, get everyone out of the house and call 911 from your cell phone.

## FIRE SAFETY—WHAT **NOT** TO DO!

Sure-fire ways to set your house ablaze while serving flaming drinks:

1. Make sure your house is chock-full of severely inebriated people and that they all crowd around as you attempt to ignite the cocktails.

2. It would be particularly good if there were a lot of women with big, heavily hairsprayed dos surrounding you.

3. A shag carpet always helps to ensure that a good fire spreads quickly.

4. By all means, try to drink the shot while it's flaming. This will not only make you "big man on campus," but it will also dramatically increase the likelihood that you'll severely burn your mouth and throat and potentially breathe fire in a manner similar to a flamethrower, setting the aforementioned hairdos and shag carpets alight. Clearly after a daring stunt like this, you would not soon be forgotten (or paroled, for that matter).

5. The surface you're working on should always be wet with alcohol from previous shooters. A beautiful blue flame will dance along the bar or table when you accidentally touch it with your match or lighter.

6. No need to bother with pesky fire extinguishers. They're way too handy in putting out fires and are frankly not aesthetically pleasing to look at. Further, think how pretty your house will be when it's engulfed in flames. For a bevy of "hot" examples of how mood lighting can add to your party, go to YouTube.com and type "flaming shots gone wrong."

7. Only invite your dopiest friends—the ones who can't remember to stop, drop, and roll if they catch on fire. And don't forget the ones with the incredibly slow reaction times who wouldn't think to smother a fire with a wet blanket (or even call 911) before it's too late.

# MAKING THE RECIPES

You've got your materials, drinks, and safety considerations taken care of. It's time for a practice round.

## MEASURING AND MIXING

As we've mentioned, most of the drink recipes list ingredients by parts: one part this, one part that, plus a splash or dash of something else to ignite the drink or spice it up. This method not only aids the metrically challenged, but allows you to serve a drink in a different type of glassware than we recommend—say, for example, the jelly jars or Elmer Fudd juice glasses you're so fond of. Just be sure whatever glassware you're using is heatproof; otherwise, your drink and the accompanying flames could put a quick end to your party.

Important: When it comes to measuring the overproof rum, Everclear, brandy, or whiskey that you're going to ignite, follow the quantities specified in the recipe. Don't think, "Hey, the recipe calls for 1 ounce, so if I use four times as much, this'll be four times as cool!" You should also not decide, "Why use a shot glass? I'll mix a bathtub full of this stuff and set it on fire." Because you will be mistaken. And possibly eyebrowless. And maybe even homeless.

As for mixing, simply follow the recipe, adding the alcohols in the order in which they appear. If it says to stir, stir. If it tells you to layer, see Flaming Layered Shots on page 22.

*Make sure your glassware is heatproof before experimenting.

# LIGHTING 'EM UP

There are a finite number of ways to ignite a drink. The object is to keep your eyes, face, clothes, hands, and other vital parts as far away from the blazing drink as possible. To accomplish this, choose long matches, that campfire lighter with the long neck, or bamboo sticks/skewers. As mentioned previously in our discussion of lighting equipment, cocktail purists would recommend the bamboo sticks so that your artful concoction doesn't taste like burnt matches or butane. You can light the bamboo sticks/skewers with a match or lighter. Keep a large ashtray or glass of water on hand to extinguish your fire conductor once you're done.

Once your drink (or drinks) is lit, you should let everyone admire the spectacle for no more than five to ten seconds. (You'll be surprised how long that is.) At that point, you can cup the flaming shooters with an empty glass, or if you have multiple flaming shooters, gently lower a wide strip of heavy-duty aluminum foil over the row to cut off the air supply. (For advice on how to extinguish flaming punch bowls or other big vats or ladles of burning booze, see Fire Safety Tips, page 16).

# DRINKING 'EM UP

Advise anyone drinking one of your hot shots to do it quickly: they are called "shooters" not "sippers" for a reason. They should hold the glass from the bottom and avoid placing their lips directly on the rim, which may be hot!

# PUTTING IT ALL TOGETHER

Think of your bar setup as a work of art. You're preparing a piece of performance art for your guests. Your bar is your stage. Your tools are your set. And you are the leading lady or gent. To be safe, consider this a solo production; however you should enlist the help of your most faithful, levelheaded friend to act as your trusty assistant and fire marshal. Your audience should offer the proper reverence to you and the flames. They should be attentive but keep their distance. The fire marshal must ensure the "front row" is free of people (and anything else that could easily catch on fire.

Start with a clean bar or work surface. Line your shooters or cocktail glasses artfully. Ensure you have appropriate fire-extinguishing accoutrements. Mix, layer, shake, and pour your cocktails with as much flare as you can muster. Consider offering a witty toast prior to setting your drinks ablaze.

With your elegant and visually interesting bar in place, your drinks mixed, your fire marshal primed, your guests rapt, it's time to make fire. Dim the lights so that your flames are easily visible. Once you've put the flames out, invite your audience to join you "on stage" to enjoy their exotic drinks. You have just started your party with an unforgettable flare. Now you can kick back and enjoy yourself.

# BARTENDING TRICKS & TECHNIQUES

f you want to look like a polished bartending pro with little effort and even less training, then these techniques are your secret weapon. Master them and you'll look like hot stuff. Fail and you could get your whiskers singed. A technique icon (see page 28) will appear with each recipe, so if flaming zests or the cement mixer is the next technique you want to tackle, you can easily locate recipes that use them.

## STATS

Skill Level:

Serve In:

Danger:

Technique:

Potency:

## FLAMING SHOTS

This is the simplest flaming drink to execute, but the wow factor is very high. You add spirits and liqueurs to a shot or rocks glass in whatever proportions the recipes calls for. You float your flaming agent on top (typically 151-proof rum or Everclear, and never more than an ounce), then you ignite the rum with a long match or lit skewer. Enjoy the blaze for a few seconds—if you let it burn too long, you'll burn off most of the alcohol. The best way to extinguish the flame: Simply place an empty shot or rocks glass over the flaming shot. You can also blow out the flame. Just be sure that the flame is thoroughly extinguished before you drink; in bright light, burning alcohol is very difficult to see, so dim the lights if you are unsure.

# FLAMING LAYERED SHOTS

The number-one rule of layering drinks (flaming or otherwise): Choose the heaviest liqueur for your bottom layer and build on up to the lightest. If you're making a hot shot, last of all comes the alcohol you plan to ignite. Float it gently on top so as not to wreck your layered effect.

Here are some more tips on making successful layered drinks:

- Check the size of your glass to make sure it's large enough. You wouldn't want to fill the glass after layer two, when your recipe calls for four luscious layers.
- Pour each of the liqueurs or spirits slowly and steadily over the back of a spoon. (The rounded side of the spoon should face up; the tip of the spoon should touch the insides of the glass, just above the previous layer.) This technique slows the liqueur down and distributes it evenly over the layer below it.
- Keep the glass very still while you pour. If you bump it, your layers will collapse—all that hard work for nothing!

Our recipes for layered drinks list the liqueurs in order—from the heavyweights to the featherweights. But after trying a few of them, you may want to create variations—or entirely original—layered drinks of your own. Check out A Handy Guide to Layering Liqueurs on page 23, which, for your convenience, organizes common varieties by their specific gravities (weight) in descending order.

# A HANDY GUIDE TO LAYERING LIQUEURS

Here are some common liqueurs organized by density, from heaviest (this is your first layer) to lightest (this is your last layer). Easy peasy!

Grenadine
Crème de cassis
Anisette
Kahlúa
Crème de banana (aka banana cream)
Coffee liqueur
Green crème de menthe
White crème de menthe
Blue curaçao
Galliano
Blackberry liqueur
Amaretto
Triple sec
Apricot liqueur
Drambuie
Frangelico
Apricot brandy
Sambuca
Blackberry brandy
Campari
Midori (melon)
Cointreau (orange)
Peppermint schnapps
Kümmel
Peach schnapps
Sloe gin
Brandy
Green Chartreuse
Southern Comfort
Kirsch

**Please note:** Sugar contents and flavoring agents—and thus densities—vary a little from brand to brand. So, for a completely reliable presentation, experiment with any layered extravaganza before you serve it to guests.

# THE SLAM DUNK

Here's an oldie but a goodie. You fill a shot glass with some sweet stuff and add a splash of some overproof stuff. Light the shot and then extinguish the flame by dropping the lit shot into a glass three-quarters full of beer (of course). Enjoy the attention that will surely follow, and invite one of your guests to slam it. Repeat. The Flaming Dr. Pepper (and all its different formulas) is perhaps the most famous slam-dunking drink of them all.

# FLAMING ZEST

This technique isn't difficult to master, and it literally creates sparks. You cut a wide strip of zest from an orange, lemon, or grapefruit (for best results, we recommend a big navel orange). Hold the zest between your thumb and forefinger, and gently warm it with a lighter for a few seconds. Then pinch the zest so that its oil squirts through the flame. You'll see a flash as the oil ignites. How amazing are you?! But, don't lose your cool just yet. Finish by swiping the zest around the rim of the glass and offering the drink to that hottie you've had your eye on all night.

# FLAMING SUGAR CUBE

This clever technique takes advantage of the flame's unique ability to turn a sugar cube into an irresistibly caramelized spoonful of burnt sugar. The sugar cube (or a spoonful of sugar) is doused with a little 151-proof rum or Everclear. The spoon is balanced on a rocks glass while the alcohol-soaked sugar is ignited. Let the flames burn until the sugar begins to solidify and caramelize, then dunk the spoon into the glass and stir rapidly to extinguish the flames. If you love the flavor of caramelized sugar, you'll enjoy the Flaming Lemon Drop and Apple Passion, which both employ this technique.

# THE CEMENT MIXER

We're not sure if this technique has an official name, but we call it the cement mixer because the rotating motion reminds us of a cement truck. Despite the lowbrow name, this technique will impress even your most sophisticated guests. Here's how it works: You add some overproof alcohol to a brandy snifter, ignite it, then *slowly and carefully* rotate the snifter like a cement mixer until the flames burn themselves out (or until you *very carefully* pour the contents of the snifter into another glass). The rotation will warm the alcohol evenly without shattering the glass that contains it. To make the cement-mixer motion easier to execute, balance the brandy snifter horizontally on a rocks glass before you ignite the alcohol with a long match or lit skewer.

# BLAZING CUPS

Jerry Thomas, a bartender at the El Dorado Saloon in San Francisco, who is revered as the godfather of modern-day mixology, invented this spectacular technique, featured in a drink known as the Blue Blazer. Listen to a description of this technique and you'll understand why: Heat two silver-lined tankards by filling them with hot water. In one, combine boiling water and sugar, stirring to dissolve. In the other pour warm whiskey. Ignite the whiskey, and while it's still blazing, pour the flaming whiskey into the hot water tankard, then back into the original tankard. Pour the mixture back and forth a few times, partially to mix the drink, but primarily for the drama of the blazing blue alcohol shooting back and forth between the mugs. (If you were Jerry Thomas, you would carefully increase the distance between the mugs each time you pour, but you're not, so don't showboat.)

Once the drink is thoroughly mixed (or you've received enough attention), garnish it with a lemon peel and serve in one of the tankards, or pour into what's known as a London dock glass—a stemmed port glass that also works well for hot mixed drinks. We share this technique because it's an awe-inspiring bit of flaming cocktail history, but you need not try it at home. Instead consider ordering this classic the next time you're at a swish cocktail bar, though even your bartender may back away from this mixological feat!

# FLAMING PUNCH BOWL OR CHAFING DISH

This book finishes with a chapter called Blazing Punches for Festive Frolics, which contains an assortment of traditional flaming punches. In order to make a flaming punch, you'll need a heatproof punch bowl or a chafing dish and a lid that's large enough to cover it completely. A chafing dish is one of those metal containers with a heat source directly under it that you see on hotel buffet tables. A chafing dish will keep your punch warm; a punch bowl will look more festive, but could shatter if the contents get too hot (unfortunately even if it's heatproof), so most of the recipes in this book employ a chafing dish. You can pick up one for cheap at a tag sale or on eBay.

Sometimes you touch a long match or lit skewer to the surface of the punch and ignite the whole bowlful. More often, you ignite some booze in a long-handled ladle, then stir the ladle into the punch to extinguish the flames. Just remember that your punch bowl or chafing dish probably already contains a lot of alcohol, so when you plunge the ladle in, that alcohol might catch fire, too. Quickly extinguish the flames with the lid. (You can borrow a lid from a stockpot or skillet, as long as it covers the punch completely.) Whatever you use, don't let the punch burn for more than a few seconds. Otherwise, too much of the alcohol will burn away, and where's the fun in that?

# HOT SHOT PROFILES AT-A-GLANCE

We want to make it as easy as possible for you to achieve your alcohol-related ambitions. So, whether your goal is to dazzle your friends with your supremely slick bartending skills or simply to knock them on their asses with shots so strong they could power a Lincoln Navigator for a week, refer to the handy icons that demystify and rank each recipe.

## SERVE IN

- shot glass (1 to 2 ounces)
- rocks glass (4 to 8 ounces)
- cocktail glass (4 ½ ounces)
- Collins glass (10 to 14 ounces)
- brandy snifter (size varies)
- Pousse-café glass (2 to 4 ounces)
- Irish coffee mug
- beer mug
- punch bowl and cups

## TECHNIQUE

- flaming shot
- flaming layered shot
- the slam dunk
- flaming zest
- flaming sugar cube
- the cement mixer
- blazing cups
- flaming punch bowl/chafing dish
- flaming ladle

## POTENCY

 lightweight friendly

 you're gonna feel it (eat a full meal first)

 wicked strong (stock up on Gatorade)

## DANGER ALERT

 alcohol + flame = danger

 you're playing with fire, dude

 keep 911 on your speed dial

## SKILL LEVEL

 virgin bartender

 budding mixologist

 extreme bartender

# FINAL FIRE-SAFETY NOTE

Extreme caution should be taken when making any of the flaming drinks featured herein. That said, the drinks branded with the skull and crossbones require a significant amount of moxie, skill, and attention to detail. You may want to leave these drinks to the professionals.

# LET'S GET THE PARTY STARTED!

**T**HIS CHAPTER OFFERS COOL RECIPES FOR HOT SHOTS THAT'LL STRIKE A SPARK UNDER ANY PARTY'S ASS. THERE ARE VARIATIONS ON CLASSICS LIKE THE B-52 AND THE DR PEPPER (WHICH REALLY *DOES* TASTE LIKE THE BOTTLED STUFF) AND LAYERED DRINKS LIKE THE FLAMING RASTA AND THE FLAMBÉ, WHICH ARE AS PRETTY AS THEY ARE POTENT. IF YOU WANT TO PUT ON A REAL MAGIC SHOW, UNVEIL THE MAD SCIENTIST, WHICH CREATES A COOL GREEN FLAME, OR PRESENT THE CARIBBEAN SMOKED TORCH, WHICH DELIVERS A POOF OF AROMATIC SMOKE. THE COOKIE MONSTER AND MORPHINE DRIP OFFER OPTIONS FOR THE SWEET TOOTHS IN THE HOUSE. JUST BE SURE YOU KNOW WHEN TO STOP POURING OR YOUR PARTY WILL QUICKLY MOVE INTO CHAPTER 3 TERRITORY: WHO WANTS TO GET SCHNOCKERED?

# FLAMING B-52

The classic B-52 features creamy layers of Kahlúa, amaretto, and Baileys Irish Cream. But there are many different models of this popular drink, some barely recognizable from the original except in their ability to make you fly high. We include the Mid-Air Collision, an aptly titled variation that is a fusion of a B-52 and a Concorde (see page 127 for recipe).

1 part Kahlúa
1 part Baileys Irish Cream
1 part amaretto almond liqueur
1 splash 151-proof rum

1. Layer ingredients in a shot glass in this order: Kahlúa, Irish Cream, and amaretto.

2. Float the 151 on top and light it.

3. Salute, extinguish the flames with an empty shot glass, and you're ready for takeoff.

## MID-AIR COLLISION VARIATION:

This shot demonstrates that there is such a thing as a happy accident. Carefully layer the components of a B-52 listed above but add 1 part coffee liqueur before the splash of 151.

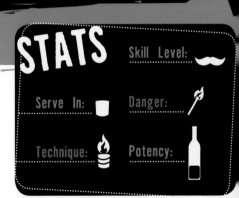

STATS

Skill Level:

Serve In:

Danger:

Technique:

Potency:

# S'MORES

Chocolate. Graham crackers. Marshmallows. Fire. Imagine all these ingredients a shot glass and you've got a very different sort of S'mores than the one the ki clamor for on camping trips. Though we can't imagine lugging all these bottl around in a backpack, this drink will remind you of a fun evening around t campfire.

1 part crème de cacao or chocolate liqueur
½ part butterscotch schnapps
½ part Baileys Irish Cream
1 splash 151-proof rum

Teddy Grahams
Mini marshmallows
Bamboo skewers

**1.** Place 2 or 3 marshmallows on the bamboo skewer.

**2.** Pour the crème de cacao, butterscotch schnapps, and Irish Cream into the shot glass. The drop a Teddy Graham into the glass.

**3.** Top off the shot with the 151. After you ignite it, roast your mini marshmallows for 5 to 1 seconds.

**4.** Extinguish the flames, knock back the shot, and follow it up with the marshmallows. If yo want, you could drop the marshmallows into the drink before consuming.

**STATS** | SERVE IN | TECHNIQUE | POTENCY | SKILL LEVEL | DANGER

# THE FOURTH OF JULY

Put on your own pyrotechnic display on Independence Day and salute this layered shot, which shows off a little of the ol' red, white, and blue. The fireworks you set off making this drink will please all onlookers. If you want more "white" and less alcohol in this drink, replace the vodka with heavy cream.

1 part grenadine
1 part vodka

1 part blue curaçao
1 splash 151-proof rum

1. Pour each drink carefully in order.
2. Float the 151 and ignite.
3. Enjoy the "oohs" and "ahhs" before fully extinguishing and drinking.

STATS | SERVE IN | TECHNIQUE | POTENCY | SKILL LEVEL | DANGER

# FLAMING RASTA

So what if you're partying on a rooftop or a suburban deck, this hot shot will transport you to a Jamaican beach with the flick of a match. This bold layered drink wears the Rasta colors with pride: the minty crème de menthe is the green of the Jamaican countryside, the deep red grenadine signifies the blood of their martyrs, and the golden Baileys stands for the wealth of Africa. Yeah, mon.

1 part grenadine
1 part Baileys Irish Cream

1 part green crème de menthe
1 splash 151-proof rum

**1.** Layer the ingredients in a shot glass in this order: grenadine, Irish Cream, crème de menthe

**2.** Float the 151 on top and light it with a match.

**3.** Extinguish by placing an empty shot glass over the flaming shot.

**4.** Toast your Rasta brothers and sisters and drink up.

STATS | SERVE IN | TECHNIQUE | POTENCY | SKILL LEVEL | DANGER

# CARIBBEAN SMOKED TORCH

Let's face it, there are a truckload of ingredients in this concoction. This is for the consummate host or hostess, throwing a tropical-themed barbeque for sophisticated, jet-setting friends. If you fit this description, read on.... The flamed rum in the snifter, followed by the aromatic puff of smoke will delight your well-heeled friends and act as a refreshing compliment to your jerk chicken! For tips on the Cement Mixer technique used in this recipe, see page 25. P.S.: You'll want to practice this one before game day!

½ ounce brandy
¾ ounce Midori melon liqueur
¾ ounce raspberry liqueur
¾ ounce coconut rum
½ ounce dark rum
1 ounce cranberry juice
1 ounce orange juice
1 ounce pineapple juice
½ ounce 151-proof rum

1. Combine all of the ingredients except the 151-proof rum in a cocktail shaker with crushed ice.

2. Shake until chilled. Pour the 151-proof rum in a brandy snifter and ignite it.

3. Carefully warm the snifter with the rum, rotating it slowly like a cement mixer, until the rum burns itself out.

4. When the rum is extinguished, pour the contents of the shaker into the hot snifter.

5. If you do it right, you'll create a deliciously fragrant cloud of smoke!

## STATS

| SERVE IN | TECHNIQUE | POTENCY | SKILL LEVEL | DANGER |
|---|---|---|---|---|
|  |  |  |  |  |

# FLAMING BLAZER

For the cowboy with a heart of gold, the Flaming Blazer appears. Southern Comfort instantly boosts your testosterone by challenging your liver to a fight. The crème de cacao takes the edge off the whiskey, much like how the love of a good woman can tame the beast in a man. Finally, by lighting this on fire, you show the world you are your own man . . . rugged and strong like every good cowboy should be.

part white crème de cacao
part Southern Comfort
part 151-proof rum

1. Pour the crème de cacao and Southern Comfort into a shot glass neat.

2. Float the 151 on top, light it with a match (in our opinion, it'd be sexy if you'd strike the match on your boot), and let it blaze.

3. Extinguish by placing an empty shot glass over the flaming shot glass, then shoot.

# FLAMING LEMON DROP

This old standby started out as a shooter. The flaming lemon slice, which is topped with sugar, soaked in 151, and ignited, is a real spectacle. And, after the flames go out, you get to down your shot, lick the sugar, and suck the lemon in whatever order you prefer—just be sure to give the sugar a couple seconds to cool off. Caramelized = hot! You can use unflavored vodka, but Absolut Citron makes for an especially lemony drink.

1 shot lemon vodka
1 splash Galliano herbal liqueur (optional)
1 lemon wheel

¼ teaspoon sugar
2 dashes 151-proof rum

1. Pour a shot of lemon vodka, add a splash of Galliano, if desired, and then cover the top of the shot glass with the lemon wheel.

2. Sprinkle the sugar on top of the lemon, and then soak the sugar with the 151.

3. Ignite the rum and let it burn until the sugar is caramelized.

4. Thoroughly blow out the flame, and allow a few seconds of anticipation before you slam your shot, lick your sugar, and suck that lemon wheel. Yum!

STATS

| SERVE IN | TECHNIQUE | POTENCY | SKILL LEVEL | DANGER |

# SOUTHERN BOUND METEOR

The cherry and flecks of gold from the Goldschläger create a feast for the eyes with this shooter. It's a great way to start off the evening in a fun, festive manner.

If you happen to be flanked by a gaggle of models, this is the perfect drink. It can be your first drink and their dinner. Who said models were high maintenance?

1 maraschino cherry

1 part Southern Comfort

1 part Goldschläger

1 splash 151-proof rum

**1.** Remove the stem from a cherry and drop it in a shot glass.

**2.** Pour in the Southern Comfort and the Goldschläger neat.

**3.** Float the 151 on top and ignite it.

**4.** Enjoy the pretty sparkles; then extinguish by placing an empty shot glass over the flaming shot glass.

**5.** Offer the cherry to one of your (no doubt hungry) companions, and then consume your shot.

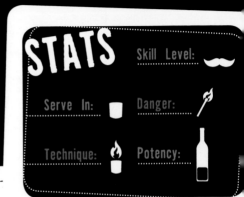

## STATS

Skill Level:

Serve In:

Danger:

Technique:

Potency:

# FLAMING MEXICAN FLAG

Cinco de Mayo is the flag-waving holiday in honor of the outnumbered Mexican army's surprising defeat of Napoleon's mighty French aggressors in the Battle of Puebla on May 5, 1862. Ironically the holiday is celebrated more fervently in the States than in Mexico. A festive, bright-colored shot, this is perfect for celebrating independence. You may want to line your stomach with a quesadilla or two prior to downing this one though.

1 part grenadine

1 part green crème de menthe

1 part tequila blanco

1 part 151-proof rum

1. Layer in a shot glass in this order: grenadine, crème de menthe, and tequila.

2. Float the 151 on top.

3. Ignite it.

4. Shout, "Viva México!" before extinguishing the flames with an empty shot glass then knocking back the shot.

## STATS

Skill Level:

Serve In:

Danger:

Technique:

Potency:

# EVERYBODY'S IRISH

You don't have to wait for St. Patty's Day to serve this one. In fact, after a couple o rounds, your guests (Irish or not) may take to the streets for an impromptu parade

2 parts whiskey
½ part green crème de menthe

1. Pour the whiskey and crème de menthe into a shot glass neat (see Tip).

2. Light the whiskey and enjoy your St. Patty's Day parade in a glass.

3. Extinguish the flame by placing an empty shot glass over the flaming shot, then toss it back.

## TIP:

Whiskey is typically 80 proof. If you have trouble lighting the first round, warm the glasses in hot water before adding the booze.

STATS

Skill Level:

Serve In:

Danger:

Technique:

Potency:

# GODZILLA BREATH

There are several shots and cocktails bearing the name Godzilla, but this is the one we feel best represents the King of the Monsters. Knock back a couple of these, and you'll be ready to take on any tiny army that's in your way.

1 part vodka
1 part Mountain Dew (chilled)
2-4 drops Tabasco sauce
1 splash 151-proof rum

1. Combine the vodka and Mountain Dew in a shot glass and then add the Tabasco sauce.

2. Float the 151 on top and ignite.

3. Do your best Godzilla dance before blowing out the flames and drinking.

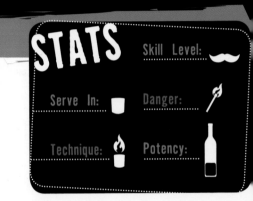

STATS

Skill Level:

Serve In:

Danger:

Technique:

Potency:

# FLAMING GIRL SCOUT COOKIE

This drink, also known as an After Five, is sweet, minty, and smooth. Perfect for an after-dinner treat. We added the flame just for kicks. Not recommended for actual girl scouts.

part coffee liqueur
part Baileys Irish Cream
part peppermint schnapps
splash 151-proof rum

1. Pour the coffee liqueur into a shot glass.
2. Carefully layer the Irish Cream and then the schnapps.
3. Float the 151-proof rum on top and ignite.
4. Extinguish the flames before consuming.

## STATS

Skill Level:

Serve In:

Danger:

Technique:

Potency:

# FLAMING DR PEPPER

If you and your friends want to toss back something more creative than your typical Saturday night 12-pack, here's a drink that delivers those brews with a twist. There are many versions of this classic drink, all claiming to taste just like the soda. We think this simple formula is pretty convincing. (In fact, the more of it you drink, the more convinced you'll be!) But if you want to experiment, check out the more subtle concoction below.

3 parts amaretto almond liqueur
1 part 151-proof rum

1 bottle (12 ounces) beer

**1.** Pour the amaretto into a shot glass and top it off with the 151.

**2.** Ignite the rum.

**4.** After it's burned a few seconds—long enough to get everyone's attention—extinguish the shot by dropping it into the beer.

## VARIATION:

Fill a shot glass half full with amaretto, and then add 2 parts Kahlúa and 1 part root beer schnapps. Float 1 part overproof rum on top. Proceed to Step 2.

**STATS**

Skill Level:

Serve In:        Danger:

Technique:        Potency:

# HAKKESPETT

What better way to jumpstart a party than a German drink connected to a completely nonsensical ritual? (At least we think it's nonsense, but maybe it seems perfectly rational if you're from Germany.) We won't give away all the details, but it involves wet palms and peckers . . . woodpeckers, that is. Curious? Read on.

1 ½ ounces Cointreau orange-flavored liqueur
1 ½ ounces green Chartreuse

1. Layer the Cointreau and Chartreuse in a rock's glass.

2. Tilt slightly to make it easy to light the mixture with a long match.

3. Wet your palm (lick it or use a damp rag if your spit might offend) and quickly place it over the top of the glass to create a seal until the fire goes out. (You don't burn yourself if you hand is wet, you are quick, and the seal is tight. Got it?)

4. Ready for your drink? Give the glass a little shake, slowly remove your hand, and then inhale the air inside the glass before slamming the contents.

5. Here comes the nonsense part: As soon as your drink is gone, put two fingers in your mouth, inhale really fast, and attempt to say: *"Hakkespett!"* This is German for "woodpecker." Don't ask us why, just say it!

STATS | SERVE IN | TECHNIQUE | POTENCY | SKILL LEVEL | DANGER

# FLAMBÉ

This striking layered shot sets the stage for a sophisticated soiree or makes you look like a bartending maverick any night of the week. For tips on layering with finesse, see page 22.

| | |
|---|---|
| 1 part grenadine | 1 part vodka |
| 1 part white crème de menthe | 1 part 151-proof rum |

1. Carefully layer the ingredients in a shot glass in this order: grenadine, crème de menthe, and vodka.

2. Float the 151 on top, light it, and enjoy the spectacle.

3. Extinguish the flame by placing an empty shot glass over the shot.

4. Toast your own bartending genius, then drink up.

**STATS**

| SERVE IN | TECHNIQUE | POTENCY | SKILL LEVEL | DANGER |
|---|---|---|---|---|

# MAD SCIENTIST

So what if you were a geek in high school? Your hours in the chemistry lab will make you the life of the party today. This flaming cocktail creates an eerie green flame that'd make any evil genius proud. Better still, it tastes a lot like a Jolly Rancher of the "hot apple" persuasion. Midori, a bright green, melon-flavored liqueur, is the secret ingredient. (But you don't have to tell them that.)

2 ounces Midori melon liqueur
1½ ounces sour mix

1 splash soda water
¼ teaspoon 151-proof rum

1. Combine Midori, sour mix, and soda water with crushed ice in a cocktail shaker.

2. Shake and strain into a cocktail glass.

3. Float the 151 on top.

4. Ignite it.

5. Enjoy the phosphorescent green glow before you thoroughly blow out the flames.

6. Sample your potion.

STATS

Skill Level:

Serve In: 

Danger: 

Technique: 

Potency:

# BRANDED NIPPLE

It can't be denied, everyone loves saying the word "nipple." Here you'll find a titillating twist on the old classic known as the Slippery Nipple.

Perfect for ladies' night out, bachelorette parties, or for a pack of cougars out on the town, this racy drink is guaranteed to get the attention of revelers of the male persuasion.

1 part Baileys Irish Cream
1 part Goldschläger

1 part butterscotch schnapps
1 splash 151-proof rum

1. Carefully layer the ingredients in a shot glass in this order: Irish Cream, Goldschläger, and butterscotch schnapps. (The Goldschläger will add pretty flecks of gold leaf and an intense cinnamon flavor.)

2. Float the 151 on top.

3. Light it on fire.

4. Thoroughly blow out the flames before you indulge in this racy shot.

| STATS | SERVE IN | TECHNIQUE | POTENCY | SKILL LEVEL | DANGER |
|-------|----------|-----------|---------|-------------|--------|

# MORPHINE DRIP

A diagnosis of agonizing pain is not a prerequisite for a dose of this Morphine Drip. In fact, all the patients at your party can enjoy this sweet almond- and butterscotch-flavored shot. We always say all the best medicines taste like candy!

1 part amaretto almond liqueur
1 part butterscotch schnapps

1 splash 151-proof rum

1. Pour the amaretto and butterscotch schnapps into a shot glass.

2. Float the 151 on top.

3. Light it on fire.

4. Extinguish with an empty shot glass before self-medicating.

5. Wait at least a few minutes before checking your symptoms to determine whether you need another dose.

## STATS

| SERVE IN | TECHNIQUE | POTENCY | SKILL LEVEL | DANGER |
|----------|-----------|---------|-------------|--------|

# COOKIE MONSTER

This cool-looking layered drink is easy to make and tastes delicious. Designed for a woman, but strong enough for a man, it's a good way to let everyone know you're serious about partying. But given the relatively low proof, you can expect it will be a long night!

1 part Kahlúa
1 part Baileys Irish Cream

1 teaspoon 151-proof rum

1. In a shot glass layer the Kahlúa and Baileys Irish Cream.

2. Finish with the 151 and ignite it.

3. Extinguish by placing an empty shot glass over your flaming shot.

4. Enjoy. Like milk and cookies in a shot glass. Mmmm!

STATS

Skill Level:

Serve In:

Danger:

Technique:

Potency:

# FLAMING ROCK STAR

You're in Vegas, and against everyone's better judgment, you and your friends blew the doors out on your first night. Of course you did, it's Vegas! It's time to rally for the main event, the real reason you came . . . insert name of Bachelor/Bachelorette or Birthday Boy or Girl here: _____.

Start your evening off with a fun flaming flare. The dancing flame atop this drink signals the party has officially begun. Yet the Red Bull and the relatively low alcohol content help to prepare the already battered liver for the bender that's sure to follow!

½ ounce gin
½ ounce Grand Marnier orange liqueur
½ ounce coconut rum
½ ounce orange-flavored vodka
3 ounces Red Bull
3 ounces sour mix
1 splash 151-proof rum
1 orange slice

1. Combine all of the ingredients except the 151 and the orange slice in a cocktail shaker with crushed ice.

2. Shake, and then strain into a Collins glass.

3. Add 151 and the orange slice, and fire it up.

4. Thoroughly blow out the flames, then indulge. Who's a rock star now?

**STATS**

| SERVE IN | TECHNIQUE | POTENCY | SKILL LEVEL | DANGER |
|----------|-----------|---------|-------------|--------|
|  |  |  |  |  |

# FLAMING JELLY BEAN

Pay homage to your favorite Greek friends with the use of the anise-flavored ouzo. This is a fun unisex drink to get a party going or to enjoy before a night out. You can serve with sweets or as a way to segue from dinner to fiesta time.

1 part blackberry brandy

1 part 151-proof rum

1 part ouzo

1. Combine the blackberry and the ouzo in a shot glass.
2. Float the 151 on top.
3. Light it up.
4. Extinguish completely.
5. Bottoms up!

STATS

| SERVE IN | TECHNIQUE | POTENCY | SKILL LEVEL | DANGER |

# WHO WANTS TO GET SCHNOCKERED?

I f your answer is, "You and me and everyone we know," you've turned to the right chapter. The drinks that follow are mainly shooters with relatively high proofs. Some are simple and easy to execute, such as Flaming Fruit Trees, Flaming Licorice, and Pyro. Others require a skilled hand to accomplish the visual wonder that is a layered shot, with bright contrasting colors smartly stacked as in the Flaming Blue Jesus and Feel the Burn. We also pay homage to everyone's favorite loser, Homer Simpson, with the Flaming Moe.

So, when you know you're in it for the long haul for occasions like bachelor/bachelorette parties, twenty-fifth or thirtieth birthday parties, I Can't Believe He/She Dumped Me! nights out on the town, or any other situation that makes you itch to feel that tipsy warm glow, turn to the recipes herein.

# WORDS OF WISDOM FROM VETERAN DRINKERS

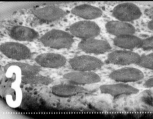

1. Eat bread a few hours before the big blowout.

2. Stock the fridge with Gatorade or Pedialyte.

3. Order a pizza before you go out, so it's there when you get home.

4. For God's sake, read the fire safety section on page 14.

5. If you're making these drinks at home, practice before you flame!

# FLAMING BLUE JESUS

You may come across a couple takes on the Flaming Jesus. All are high proof, hair-on-your-chest concoctions designed to put you well on your way to drunkdom. Careful, methinks too many of these will have mere mortals praying to the Porcelain Jesus before too long!

| | |
|---|---|
| part peppermint schnapps | 1 part tequila |
| part Southern Comfort | 1 part 151-proof rum |

1. Layer in a shot glass in this order: peppermint schnapps, Southern Comfort, and tequila.

2. Float the 151 on top.

3. Light it up, and let it burn bright.

4. Extinguish with an empty shot glass, toss it back, and repeat until you experience your own personal resurrection.

## VARIATION:

This Flaming Jesus version features equal parts vodka, lime juice, grenadine, and 151. It may not be blue, but it has the power to make you praise the Lord.

**STATS**

Skill Level:

Serve In: Danger:

Technique: Potency:

# ANGRY CATHOLIC

If Sunday morning has always meant Mass, no matter how hungover you were, pick another tonic. But if you were the sneaky altar boy who sampled the wine when the priest wasn't looking, or the naughty schoolgirl who wore garters under her skirt and smoked Camels in the confession booth, then bottoms up—you are an angry Catholic and this drink is for you!

1 ounce tequila
1 or 3 drops Tabasco sauce (depending on how angry you are)
1 splash 151-proof rum

1. Pour the tequila into a shot glass neat.

2. Add the drops of Tabasco and watch them sink to the bottom of the glass.

3. Float the 151 on top.

4. Ignite it.

5. Thoroughly blow out the flame.

6. Slam it. Best enjoyed with other angry Catholics.

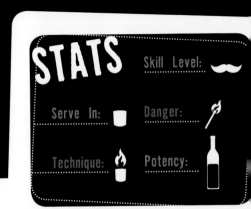

STATS

Skill Level:

Serve In:

Danger:

Technique:

Potency:

# BLAZING SADDLE

When it's time to kick off your allegorical spurs and remove that metaphorical ten-gallon hat, invite Johnson, Johnson, and your other buddy Johnson over for some o these badass shots. The real cowboys may drink from a flask, but there's no reason you can't enjoy a few fireworks before you get s#*tfaced.

3 parts blackberry brandy
1 part 151-proof rum

**1.** Pour the brandy into a shot glass.

**2.** Top with 151.

**3.** Ignite and enjoy the show.

**4.** Blow it out completely before slamming it.

**5.** Sidle up to the bar for another round.

## STATS

| SERVE IN | TECHNIQUE | POTENCY | SKILL LEVEL | DANGER |
|----------|-----------|---------|-------------|--------|

# VOLCANO

It's just like you they teach you in geology class: 151 plus Everclear makes the earth move. Add some cola and lime juice for a cocktail so refreshing you may not notice the seismic activity until it's too late.

**Note:** If Everclear is not available where you live, consider relocating.

---

1 tablespoon (more or less) lime juice

1 part 151-proof rum

1 part cola

1 splash Everclear

---

1. Add lime juice to a rocks glass, then equal parts rum and cola.

2. Float the Everclear on top.

3. Ignite it, and witness the lava-like glow.

4. Extinguish by placing an empty rocks glass over the flaming one.

5. Toss back your drink.

6. Repeat and you *will* get schnockered.

STATS

| SERVE IN | TECHNIQUE | POTENCY | SKILL LEVEL | DANGER |

# FLAMING DRAGON

Green Chartreuse has a long and legendary history. According to that venerable source of knowledge, Wikipedia, it's a secret combination of 130 herbs, flowers, and mysterious spices. The recipe is said to have been passed from François Hanniba d'Estrees to the Carthusian monks who lived at the base of the French Alps in the sixteenth century, and they have been bottling it ever since. Commonly referred to as the elixir of long life, some who have sampled Green Chartreuse claim it tastes like "burning." Others say it's akin to drinking Listerine. You've been warned!

1 part green Chartreuse
1 part 151-proof rum

**1.** Pour the Chartreuse and 151 into a shot glass neat.

**2.** Light the 151.

**3.** Let the flames warm the concoction before you extinguish them.

**4.** Drink up, and let us know how you'd describe the flavor. You may need to have a few Flaming Dragons before you develop a clear impression. (Or you may decide immediately that i tastes like mouthwash.)

## VARIATION:

Known as Flaming Dragon Snot, this version gets its green color from crème de menthe rather than Chartreuse, and the snot is neatly represented by Baileys Irish Cream: 1 part of each plus a splash of 151 and you're good to go. (Our apologies if this recipe ruins the appeal of Baileys for you forever.)

**STATS**

Skill Level:

Serve In:

Danger:

Technique:

Potency:

# FLAMING ANGRY DRAGON

Here's another dragon drink, but this one's pissed off! It features Hpnotiq, which is a blue liqueur made from vodka, cognac, and tropical fruit juices. It was created in 2001 by Raphael Yakoby, who at the time, was a college dropout living with his parents. Needless to say Yakoby's now a millionaire. Maybe the dragon's angry because he didn't come up with this idea first!

1 part Hpnotiq liqueur
1 part vodka
½ part grenadine

½ part Baileys Irish Cream
½ part Everclear or 151-proof rum

1. Mix together the Hqnotiq and vodka.

2. Layer the grenadine on top of the mixture. And then layer the Baileys.

3. Float the Everclear on top, light it up, extinguish thoroughly, then drink!

STATS

Skill Level:

Serve In:

Danger:

Technique:

Potency:

# FLAMING GOAT

Forget the goat, this drink's purple! It's also a strong drink that you'll want to be careful with.

| | |
|---|---|
| 1 part vodka | 1 part tequila |
| 1 part rum | 1 splash sour mix |
| 1 part triple sec | ½ part 151-proof rum |
| 1 part blue curaçao | |

1. Mix all the ingredients except for the overproof rum in a Collins glass.

2. Fill the glass with ice cubes.

3. Float the overproof rum on top.

4. Light the drink, admire its strange coloring, and extinguish thoroughly before drinking.

**STATS**

Skill Level:

Serve In:

Danger:

Technique:

Potency:

# FLAMING FRUIT TREES

This drink is full of contradictions. It conjures images of a dinner party with Doris Day, Snookie from the Jersey Shore, Slash from Guns N' Roses, and Richard Simmons (for extra fruity flavor). If you run with a motley crew like this, why not celebrate their differences with this fruity shooter with an edge?

1 part peach schnapps
1 part banana crème liqueur

1 part 151-proof rum

1. Pour the schnapps and banana crème into a shot glass neat.

2. Float the 151 on top.

3. Ignite, and enjoy the pretty flame.

4. Extinguish by placing an empty shot glass over the flaming shot. *Vive la différence!*

STATS

Skill Level:

Serve In:

Danger:

Technique:

Potency:

# ADIOS MOTHERF*%@ER

Do you fantasize about the day you'll walk out that door, shouting this unambiguous kiss-off to your nitpicking boss or good-for-nothing lover? Pound a few of these power-packed shots with some pals, and your dream may become a reality. The ingredients list may be long, but trust us, "screw you" never tasted so good.

3 ounces sour mix
½ ounce light rum
½ ounce blue curaçao
½ ounce vodka
½ ounce tequila blanco
½ ounce gin
⅓ ounce 7 Up
⅔ ounce 151-proof rum

1. Combine the entire slew of ingredients except the 151 in a Collins glass filled with crushed ice.

2. Float the 151 on top.

3. Ignite it, fantasizing about your glorious exit as you watch it burn.

4. Thoroughly blow out the flame and drink without stirring.

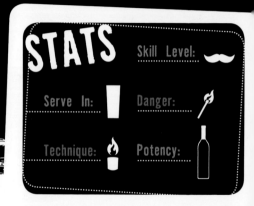

STATS

Serve In:

Technique:

Skill Level:

Danger:

Potency:

# FLAMING ASSHOLE

Despite its vulgar name, the Flaming Asshole, with its brilliant colors and swee flavors, is a tasty treat. Envision a group of fashion-forward revelers throwin a swishy, fabulous party and poking fun at the derogatory nature of this name Gays, gaggles of girls, and straight men comfortable with their sexuality could als perform a ceremonial ritual using this shooter as an elixir to ward off potenti assholes or those prone to excessive assholery.

1 part grenadine
1 part green crème de menthe

1 part banana crème liqueur
1 part 151-proof rum

**1.** Layer in a shot glass in this order: grenadine, crème de menthe, and banana crème liqueu

**2.** Float the 151 on top.

**3.** Ignite it, and say good riddance to all the assholes who have crossed your path.

**4.** Thoroughly blow out that flame and it's bottoms up!

| STATS | SERVE IN | TECHNIQUE | POTENCY | SKILL LEVEL | DANGER |
|-------|----------|-----------|---------|-------------|--------|

# A.S.S.
## ON FLAMES

aughty and nice, the A.S.S. on Flames is less menacing to drink than its moniker mplies. When you're not sure whether she likes you or your buddy, a round or two f A.S.S. on Flames should flush out her true feelings. Good luck!

1 part amaretto almond liqueur
1 part sour apple schnapps

1 part Southern Comfort
1 splash 151-proof rum

. Layer in a shot glass in this order: amaretto, schnapps, Southern Comfort.

. Carefully float the 151 on top.

. Light that A.S.S. on fire and enjoy the spectacle.

. When you get thirsty (this shouldn't take more than a few seconds), extinguish the flame and drink up.

STATS | SERVE IN | TECHNIQUE | POTENCY | SKILL LEVEL | DANGER

# BACKDRAFT

This drink is named after the phenomenon in which a fire that is starved of oxyge[n] suddenly gets some (usually by opening a door or window), often with explosiv[e] results. If you drink more than one of these, you'll also experience explosive result[s].

1 part Drambuie
1 part Grand Marnier orange liqueur

1. Pour both liqueurs into a brandy snifter.

2. Ignite, wet your palm with a damp rag, and quickly place it over the top of the glass [to] create a seal until the fire goes out. Don't worry, if you do this correctly, you won't bu[rn] yourself.

3. Slowly remove your hand, and then inhale the air inside the glass before slamming t[he] drink.

STATS | SERVE IN | TECHNIQUE | POTENCY | SKILL LEVEL | DANGER

# BACKDRAFT, THE SEQUEL

*Backdraft*, the 1991 blockbuster movie, didn't gross enough to earn a sequel, but the drink of the same name got one. The only added ingredient here is cinnamon or pepper; however, the technique is different.

---

1 part Grand Marnier orange liqueur
1-2 parts Drambuie

Cinnamon or pepper

---

. Pour the Grand Marnier into a double shot glass, and place the glass in a small bowl. Make sure the mouth of the Collins glass in step 2 can fit over the bowl.

. Pour the Drambuie into a Collins glass, swirling it around to coat the inside of the glass.

. Ignite the Drambuie and let it burn for 10 second or so.

. After the glass is warm to the touch, pour the flaming Drambuie into the shot of Grand Marnier. (That's why the shot glass is in a bowl.)

. Keep the Collins glass upside down above the flames to catch the vapor.

. Sprinkle cinnamon or pepper onto the flames for a little sparkling action.

. Put out the flames by carefully lowering the Collins glass over the shot glass and bowl.

. Remove the Collins glass once the flames are completely extinguished, quickly drop a couple of ice cubes into the Collins glass, and seal it with your hand. Shake the glass and watch the vapor condense.

. Finally, drink the shot and then slip a straw through two of your fingers and suck the vapors in the Collins glass.

| | SERVE IN | TECHNIQUE | POTENCY | SKILL LEVEL | DANGER |

# FIERY BALLS OF DEATH

If your dog died, your wife left you, the sawmill laid you off, your best friend ha pink eye because you farted on his pillow, and your mom is moving in with yo because her ex-boyfriend (your former best friend's little brother) dumped her, the drink one of these. Pair with a Swanson frozen entrée (we like Salisbury steak) an a good country tune.

1 part Triple Sec orange-flavored liqueur
1 part 151-proof rum

1. Pour the Triple Sec into a shot glass neat.

2. Float the 151 on top.

3. Ignite it.

4. As you watch it burn, envision your whole life going up in flames.

5. Extinguish the flames with an empty shot glass, drown your sorrows, and repeat.

## STATS

Skill Level:

Serve In:

Danger:

Technique:

Potency:

# FLAMING RUSSIAN

Here's a simple shooter to help you celebrate your Russian roots, real or imagined. Developed centuries ago by monks (why were monks such booze hounds?), vodka was once used for medicinal purposes. These days we have proper prescription drugs, so we might as well use this potent libation for recreational purposes, eh?

2 parts vodka
1 part 151-proof rum

1. Pour the vodka into a shot glass neat.

2. Carefully float the 151 on top.

3. Ignite it.

4. Use an empty shot glass to extinguish the flaming shot. *Na zdorovje!* (That's "To your health!" in case you don't actually speak your mother tongue.)

**STATS**

Skill Level:

Serve In:

Technique:

Danger:

Potency:

# BURNING AFRICA

We like to think the origin of this drink is the ancient African rites of passage that often demanded feats of strength and suffering through pain before one graduated from boy to man. If you're celebrating a rite of passage . . . or if you just want to get really wasted, do this shot.

part Jägermeister
part 151-proof rum

- Pour the Jägermeister and 151 in a shot glass.
- Ignite and let it glow before extinguishing.
- Toss it back.
- Congratulations! You're now officially a man—no matter what gender you were before you ingested this drink!

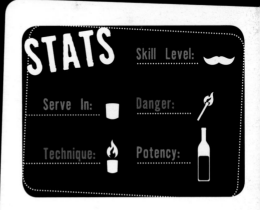

STATS

Skill Level:

Serve In:    Danger:

Technique:    Potency:

# LIGHTHOUSE

A lighthouse? Yeah, you're going to need one to navigate your sorry ass home [...] you down too many of these little jobbies. In fact, consider this drink a beacon c[...] inebriation. Serve it to fellow sailors on the *Good Ship Drunkard* who want to ge[...] lost in a raging sea of booze. Instead of igniting the usual overproof rum, this on[...] sets a little whiskey ablaze. For some added sweetness, choose a whiskey that'[...] infused with honey, like Yukon Jack.

1 part Baileys Irish Cream
1 part butterscotch schnapps
2 parts Canadian whiskey

1. Pour the Baileys and butterscotch schnapps into a shot glass neat.
2. Float the whiskey on top
3. Ignite it.
4. Extinguish by placing an empty shot glass on top of the flaming shot.
5. Ahoy, matey! You've found land.

STATS | SERVE IN | TECHNIQUE | POTENCY | SKILL LEVEL | DANGER

# FEEL THE BURN

A Greek, Kentuckian, Mexican, and an Irishman walk into a bar . . . To celebrate our nation's multicultural heritage, enjoy this drink, which boasts origins that span the globe.

part coffee liqueur
part Baileys Irish Cream
part ouzo
part Wild Turkey bourbon
part 151-proof rum

1. Layer in a shot glass in this order: coffee liqueur, Baileys Irish Cream, ouzo, and bourbon.

2. Float the 151-on top

3. Ignite it.

4. Ponder the arresting facts provided below as you watch the flame burn.

5. Extinguish and drink to the health of the Greek, the Kentuckian, and the rest of the gang in the bar.

**STATS**

| SERVE IN | TECHNIQUE | POTENCY | SKILL LEVEL | DANGER |
|----------|-----------|---------|-------------|--------|

# FUN FACTS THAT'LL MAKE YOU LOOK SMARTER THAN YOU ACTUALLY ARE:

Kentucky, the birthplace of bourbon, produces up to 95% of the world's supply of bourbon.

Circa 800 BCE: The first coffee-flavored liquor is said to have been enjoyed by Arabian kings, Roman emperors, and Egyptian pharaohs.

An early version of ouzo known as *Tsipouro* is the supposed pet project of a group of fourteenth-century monks who lived in a monastery on holy Mount Athos in Greece.

# FLAMING MELON

Unsuspecting guests beware: The Midori will likely deceive you with its pretty honeydew sweetness, while the Everclear will knock you into next Tuesday.

1 part Midori melon liqueur
1 part Everclear

1. Pour the Midori into a shot glass neat.
2. Float the Everclear on top.
3. Ignite.
4. Extinguish the flames after you've enjoyed the spectacle, then shoot.

## STATS

Serve In:

Technique:

Skill Level:

Danger:

Potency:

# FUNERAL FOR A FRIEND

Let's say you're pissed off at one of your buddies for: sleeping with your girlfriend making fun of your small penis, having alligator arms when the check comes, o for generally being a douche. This shot is a great way to take out your frustration without having to say a word. Oh, this would also be apropos for a guy who just go dumped and is looking for a relatively safe form of self-mutilation.

1 part Wild Turkey bourbon          1 part peppermint schnapps
1 part 151-proof rum

1. Pour the Wild Turkey and 151-proof rum in a shot glass so it's two-thirds full.

2. Pour the schnapps in a second chilled shot glass so it's one-third full.

3. Ignite the 151 and think of a perfect eulogy for your out-of-favor friend as you watch it burn.

4. Blow out the flame completely.

5. Pour the Wild Turkey into the schnapps, and let the funeral rites begin.

## STATS

Skill Level:

Serve In:          Danger:

Technique:          Potency:

# FLAMING COURAGE

This potent shooter will take some courage to put down, but it will give some in return. It features After Shock, a cherry-colored, cinnamon-flavored liqueur that earns its name. Good for celebrating the holidays, your Italian heritage, or that wicked cold snowmobile ride you just took, this colorful shot will liven up you and whatever party you happen to be attending.

1 part After Shock

1 part peppermint schnapps

1 part Midori melon liqueur

1 part 151-proof rum

1. Layer ingredients in a shot glass in this order: After Shock, schnapps, and Midori.

2. Float the 151 on top.

3. Ignite.

4. After the flames go out!—drink.

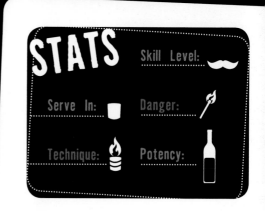

STATS

Skill Level:

Serve In:

Danger:

Technique:

Potency:

# LIQUID LUNCH

No time for a full meal? This shot will give you some of the basic food groups, long as you consider Tabasco sauce a vegetable. Do not operate heavy machine after this drink.

1 part vodka
1 part 151-proof rum
1 to 3 dashes Tabasco sauce
Pickle slice

1. Nothing fancy here. Pour the vodka and rum, to: some Tabasco sauce in, garnish with a pickle slic and light 'er up.

2. Extinguish completely before consuming. If you' still hungry, have another. Then, call it a day.

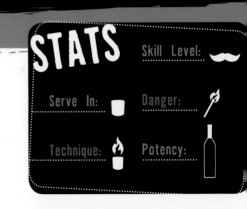

## STATS

Skill Level:

Serve In:

Danger:

Technique:

Potency:

# THE FLAMETHROWER

Grappa is made from pomace, which is pressed grape skins and seeds. In other words, it's the leftovers from winemaking. Known as a peasant's brandy, it has garnered a reputation over the years as a macho drink. Adding Southern Comfort and a flame to it doesn't hurt its reputation one bit.

- part grappa brandy
- part Southern Comfort
- splash 151-proof rum

1. Pour the grappa and Southern Comfort into a shot glass.

2. Pour the rum into a spoon and ignite.

3. Add the flaming rum to the glass . . . carefully!

4. Extinguish the flames by placing an empty shot glass over the flames.

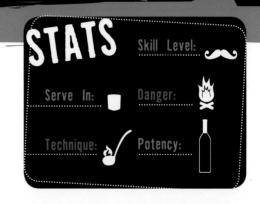

## STATS

Skill Level:

Serve In:    Danger:

Technique:    Potency:

# SWEET JESUS

Pour some shots of this peachy-sweet, oh-so-smooth libation, set them ablaze and even your most hedonistic friends will be praising the Lord like a gospel choir Sugar the rims of the glasses first and they just might speak in tongues.

1 part Southern Comfort
1 part 151-proof rum

Sugar for garnish

1. Sugar the rim of a shot glass.

2. Pour it half full of Southern Comfort.

3. Fill it with 151.

4. Ignite it.

5. Let it burn for a few seconds to warm up the contents.

6. Extinguish by placing an empty shot glass over the flaming shot.

7. Give thanks to Sweet Jesus for today's daily booze and drink up.

STATS

| SERVE IN | TECHNIQUE | POTENCY | SKILL LEVEL | DANGER |

# FLAMING MOE

Everybody loves hapless, sophomoric Homer Simpson. He occasionally, albeit surprisingly, comes up with a brilliant idea. Such was the case when he created the "Flaming Homer." Accidental ingredients, Krusty Brand Cough Syrup, and the flick of an ash from Patty's cigarette (which set the drink ablaze) greatly enhanced the flavor profile of the drink. When Homer shared his exotic concoction with local barkeep, Moe, he co-opted the drink and turned his bar into the trendiest spot in town. This of course does not last, but nonetheless serves as the inspiration for this drink (sadly the cough syrup and cigarette ash have been removed). Enjoy it with a friend you would never betray.

1 part Jägermeister

1 part crème de menthe

1 part peppermint schnapps

1 part tequila

1. Pour the ingredients into a shot glass neat.

2. Ignite it.

3. Thoroughly blow out the flame.

4. Toss it back, with a toast to Homer's health (since we all know he was the true genius behind this captivating drink).

**STATS**

| SERVE IN | TECHNIQUE | POTENCY | SKILL LEVEL | DANGER |

# FLAMING JOE

f you're the basic type who wakes up with a simple cup of Joe—no milk, no sugar, no fuss—then you should kick off a bender with an equally straightforward drink. This one features a lot of vodka to quickly get you to that inebriated place, along with a little coffee liqueur to keep you on your feet.

part coffee liqueur
parts vodka

. Pour the coffee liqueur and then the vodka into a shot glass.

. Ignite the vodka.

. Let the flame burn out completely (this should take about 10 seconds).

. Shoot.

. Repeat as needed.

STATS

| SERVE IN | TECHNIQUE | POTENCY | SKILL LEVEL | DANGER |

# FLAMING LICORICE

Nobody ever said drunks can't be cultured. This sophisticated shot features two imported liqueurs: Sambuca, which is drier than your garden-variety tipple, and Jägermeister, which is composed of an astounding number of herbs—fifty-six if you must know—plus fruits, spices, barks, resins, and then some. But the one part overproof rum ensures you'll still get as drunk as a skunk.

1 part sambuca
1 part Jägermeister

1 part 151-proof rum

1. Pour the sambuca and Jägermeister into a glass neat.

2. Float the 151 on top.

3. Ignite it, and let that licorice-y goodness burn.

4. Extinguish completely and enjoy fully.

STATS

Skill Level:

Serve In:

Danger:

Technique:

Potency:

# PYRO

you're thinking of mixing some flaming shots that list vodka, tequila, and
erproof rum as the only ingredients, then you're thinking of getting plastered.
ro can certainly help you accomplish that.

1 part vodka                    1 part 151-proof rum
1 part tequila

. Pour the ingredients into a shot glass neat.

. Ignite and then stare at the flame like any certifiable pyromaniac would.

. Extinguish by placing an empty shot glass over the flaming shot.

. Knock it back.

. Repeat if you dare!

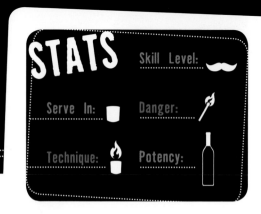

## STATS

Skill Level:

Serve In:          Danger:

Technique:         Potency:

# NAPALM

Here's a little lesson for those of you who can't distinguish the weapons of war from a cocktail: Napalm is a flammable liquid used in wartime to annihilate the enemy. This drink is a flammable liquid used in fun times to inebriate your friends. Try saying that three times fast.

1 part cinnamon schnapps
1 part vodka
1 part 151-proof rum

1. Pour the ingredients into a shot glass neat.
2. Ignite the 151 and prepare to be inebriated.
3. Extinguish the flames with an empty shot glass before consuming.

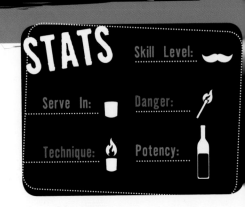

STATS

Skill Level:

Serve In:    Danger:

Technique:    Potency:

# FIRE IN THE HOLE

"Fire in the hole!" is the wartime warning used to indicate that there's about to be an explosion nearby. Don't say we didn't warn you.

1 part tequila
1 part cinnamon schnapps
1 part Jägermeister
1 splash 151-proof rum

**1.** Combine the tequila, schnapps, and Jägermeister in a shot glass.

**2.** Float the overproof rum on top and ignite.

**3.** Extinguish the flames completely before raising a glass to your brothers in arms and slamming this concoction.

STATS

Skill Level:

Serve In:       Danger:

Technique:      Potency:

# QUAFFABLE QUOTATIONS

Do not allow children to mix drinks. It is unseemly and they use too much vermouth.
–Steve Allen

Always do sober what you said you'd do drunk. That will teach you to keep your mouth shut. –Ernest Hemingway

People who drink to drown their sorrow should be told that sorrow knows how to swim.
–Ann Landers

Health: what my friends are always drinking to before they fall down.
–Phyllis Diller

When the wine goes in, strange things come out.
–Johann Christoph Friedrich von Schiller

O God, that men should put an enemy in their mouths to steal away their brains! that we should, with joy, pleasance, revel, and applause, transform ourselves into beasts!
–William Shakespeare, Othello

Once, during Prohibition, I was forced to live for days on nothing but food and water.
–W.C. Fields

The problem with some people is that when they aren't drunk, they're sober.
–William Butler Yeats

No animal ever invented anything so bad as drunkenness—or so good as drink.
–Lord Chesterton

When I read about the evils of drinking, I gave up reading.
–Henny Youngman

# IN THE MOOD FOR LOVE

**P**op in your favorite Barry White CD (or other baby-making music), light the candles, and mix up one of these sweet and sensual love potions. The Flaming Kahlúa Kiss, Apple Passion, and Flaming Banana pair nicely with sweet confections, a perfect combination for fawning over your lucky mate.

A potent cocktail with a fun twist is the Flame of Love (one of legendary crooner Dean Martin's favorites). Mastering the flaming orange peel is required, but no doubt worthwhile. Your lady friend/chap will find all that flaming citrus with sparks sexy as hell.

So, dim those lights, and in the words of Marvin Gaye, "Let's Get It On!"

# FLAMING KAHLÚA KISS

Chocolate milk with a romantic flare. If you have a fun mate and want to add some zip to your Valentine's Day dessert, try this sweet and creamy delight. It will create a memorable end to the decadent meal you've prepared for her. Pair with a chocolate soufflé, homemade chocolate chip cookies, or keep the flame theme going with some crème brûlée or s'mores!

Get your O-face and Trojans ready—this one's likely to induce lovemaking!

| | |
|---|---|
| 1 part Kahlúa | 1 part 151-proof rum |
| 1 part milk | |

1. Carefully layer the Kahlúa, milk, and 151 in a shot glass.

2. Ignite the rum.

3. Let it burn briefly.

4. Give a sly wink (you are such a stud!)

5. Blow out the shot, and offer it to your lady.

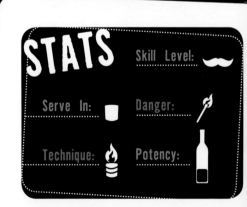

## STATS

Skill Level:

Serve In:

Danger:

Technique:

Potency:

# FLAME OF LOVE MARTINI

Legendary bartender, Pepe Ruiz, famously created this stylish concoction for Dean Martin. Pepe was a bartender at Chasen's, the place to be in the Golden Age of Hollywood. Dean's Rat Pack pal Frank Sinatra was said to be so impressed with this drink, he ordered a round for the house. To replicate this potion, you'll need to master the art of flaming orange peels, which, given the visual and aromatic delights it creates, is a worthwhile pursuit. Play "You're Nobody Till Somebody Loves You" while you dazzle your love with this potent, orange-infused martini, and prepare yourself for a fruity make-out session.

¼ teaspoon fino sherry

2 ounces vodka (save the cheap stuff for something else)

3 twists orange peel

1. Pour the sherry into a chilled cocktail glass and swirl it to coat the inside of the glass.

2. Holding the orange peel carefully between your thumb and forefinger, squeeze and express oils from the orange peel into the glass and light them with a lighter or match.

3. The burnt oil should coat the inside of the glass (see page 24 for tips on the finer points of this technique).

4. For a delectably orange-infused cocktail, repeat with the other two twists.

5. Shake the vodka with ice in a cocktail shaker.

6. Fine strain it into the coated glass.

7. Present to your paramour. You're the god/goddess of love!

STATS

Skill Level:

Serve In:

Danger:

Technique:

Potency:

# FIERY BLUE MUSTANG

Since this car first rolled off the assembly line in 1964, the Mustang has always oozed tons of sex appeal. Consider listening to songs such as Mötley Crüe's "Girls, Girls, Girls," Eddie Money's "Shakin'," or AC/DC's "You Shook Me All Night Long" while pounding this fun, blue shooter. Perfect for an '80s party. No doubt David Lee Roth would approve!

1 part banana crème liqueur
1 part blue curaçao

1 part 151-proof rum

1. Pour the banana crème and curaçao in a shot glass neat.

2. Float the 151 on top

3. Fire it up, and let it blaze.

4. Completely extinguish the shot.

5. Slam it.

6. Enjoy your ride!

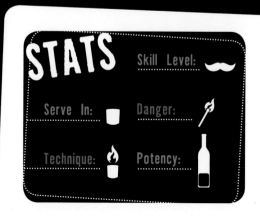

## STATS

Skill Level:

Serve In:

Danger:

Technique:

Potency:

# APPLE PASSION

Combining this forbidden fruit with a sweet dose of caramelized sugar create an unexpected delight for the senses, especially when you master this stylis presentation. Consider serving with an apple tart or panna cotta. Follow with full-body massage and then pose a question of significant import . . . When are w going to get engaged? Is it okay if I buy that new Gucci bag? My mother would lik to stay with us for the month (long pause), okay? Good luck! (Note: Rehearsal i recommended.)

| | |
|---|---|
| 1 shot apple vodka | 1 teaspoon sugar |
| ½ teaspoon Everclear | 1 shot amaretto almond liqueur |

**1.** Pour the apple vodka into a rocks glass.

**2.** Scoop the sugar into a spoon.

**3.** Balance the spoon on the rim of the rocks glass, and douse with the Everclear.

**4.** Ignite the sugar.

**5.** Once it has caramelized slightly, dunk it into the apple vodka and stir rapidly.

**6.** This will extinguish the flames and lend the drink a delicious burnt-sugar flavor.

**7.** Stir in the amaretto and enjoy!

STATS — SERVE IN | TECHNIQUE | POTENCY | SKILL LEVEL | DANGER

# FLAMING SUGAR LIPS

Silky smooth and sultry, this drink is like foreplay in a glass.

1 part vodka
1 part Baileys Irish Cream
1 part milk

½ part amaretto almond liqueur
1 splash 151-proof rum

**1.** Combine the vodka, Irish Cream, and milk with crushed ice in a cocktail shaker.

**2.** Shake and strain into a Collins glass.

**3.** Float the 151 on top and ignite it.

**4.** Thoroughly blow out the flames before giving this to the sugar lips in your life.

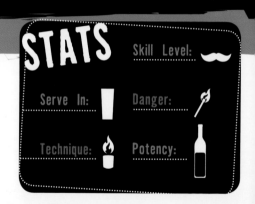

STATS

Skill Level:

Serve In:

Danger:

Technique:

Potency:

# FLAMING ORCHARD

The lemon adds a tangy tartness to this otherwise sweet-as-anything drink. The Flaming Orchard calls for sambuca as a lighting agent. If you have trouble lighting the sambuca, warm it up first by soaking a shot glass of it in a bowl of hot water first.

1 part peach schnapps
1 part Midori melon liqueur
½ part white sambuca

1 lime wheel
¼ teaspoon sugar

. Fill a shot glass with the schnapps and melon liqueur.

. Cover the top of the shot glass with the lime wheel.

. Sprinkle the sugar on top of the lime, and then soak the lime and sugar with warmed up sambuca.

. Ignite the sambuca and let it burn until the sugar is carmelized.

. Thoroughly blow out the flame, remove the lime wheel, drink the shot, and then suck on the sweet-and-sour lime.

STATS

Skill Level:

Serve In:          Danger:

Technique:         Potency:

# VOLCANIC BLAST

This pretty, layered shooter can be served to commemorate any event on the timeline of love. The spiced rum and the remnants of the 151 will produce some mild heat in your throat and tummy. Let it be surpassed only by the warmth in your loins. Hopefully your post-shooter romp stands up to the drink's name.

1 part Kahlúa
1 part Cointreau orange–flavored liqueur
1 part raspberry syrup

1 part Captain Morgan Spiced Rum
1 splash 151-proof rum

1. In a pousse-café glass, layer the ingredients as follows: Kahlúa, Cointreau, raspberry syrup, and spiced rum. (Pouring the ingredients slowly over the back of a spoon will create luscious-looking layers. For further tips on layering, see page 22.)

2. Carefully float the 151 on top.

3. Ignite your "volcano" and enjoy the spectacle.

4. Extinguish by placing an empty glass over the flaming glass.

5. Let the pousse-café glass cool for a few seconds before sipping its contents.

STATS | SERVE IN | TECHNIQUE | POTENCY | SKILL LEVEL | DANGER

# FLAMING BANANA

We could make countless innuendoes about the name of this drink. Instead we'll just say that if your partner's banana has been doing nothing but hanging out on its branch, this sweet hot shot may be the love potion for you. Mix up a batch, set it on fire, and see what comes up.

part banana crème liqueur
part black sambuca

1. Layer the banana crème and sambuca in a shot glass.
2. Ignite with a match or lighter to create your Flaming Banana.
3. Coyly blow out the flames and offer this sexy concoction to your partner.

## TIP:

If you have any trouble igniting the Sambuca, warm the glass with hot water before you fill it. The warmth will help the spirits ignite.

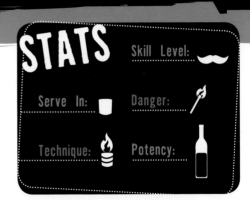

STATS

Skill Level:

Serve In:

Danger:

Technique:

Potency:

# BANANAS FOSTER LOVE POTION

Sweet and yummy, this drink is a great way to close a jovial dinner party or intimate date. The flavors of the banana, butterscotch, and rum marry well together and are further enhanced by the creamy vanilla ice cream. Make a naughty wish as you blow out the flames. If the object of your affection meets your sultry gaze with a devilish smile, chances are your dreams will come true.

| | |
|---|---|
| 1 banana | 1 ounce banana crème liqueur |
| 1 scoop vanilla ice cream | ½ ounce butterscotch schnapps |
| 1 ounce heavy cream | 1 ½ ounces dark rum |

1. Peel and slice the banana and put it in a blender, reserving one slice for garnish.

2. Add the ice cream, heavy cream, banana crème, butterscotch schnapps, and 1 ounce of the dark rum.

3. Blend to a creamy texture and pour into a brandy snifter.

4. Float the remaining ½ ounce dark rum on top and place the reserved banana slice on the rim of the glass.

5. Using a long match, ignite the rum for "wow" factor as you serve.

6. Thoroughly blow out the flame before inviting that special someone to dig in.

**STATS**

| SERVE IN | TECHNIQUE | POTENCY | SKILL LEVEL | DANGER |
|---|---|---|---|---|
|  |  |  |  |  |

# FLAMING
# BLACK RUSSIAN

You don't have to be part of a nefarious secret brotherhood to enjoy this classic drink. But a dark trench coat, the suggestion of a dangerous past, and a voice like gravel might make your leading lady swoon. Typically served on the rocks in a chilled glass, this version turns up the heat instead.

1 part Kahlúa
1 part Baileys Irish Cream

1 part vodka
1 splash 151-proof rum

1. In a shot glass, layer the ingredients in the following order: Kahlúa, Baileys, and vodka.

2. Float the 151 on top, ignite it, and watch it blaze for a few seconds.

3. Extinguish by placing an empty shot glass over the flaming glass.

4. Shoot.

5. The creamy Kahlúa at the bottom of the glass will be the last flavor you'll taste.

**STATS**

| SERVE IN | TECHNIQUE | POTENCY | SKILL LEVEL | DANGER |

# THE FLAMING BEACON

If you're so smitten that no metaphor is too corny, then layer this in a pair of shot glasses, light 'em up, and proclaim to your lover that she's your lighthouse in a storm, your beacon in the night—you are completely lost at sea without her. If she loves you, she'll love the gesture. If not, these shots are pretty potent: Keep slamming them until you no longer feel the pain of unrequited love.

| | |
|---|---|
| 1 part Kahlúa | 1 part 151-proof rum |
| 1 part Baileys Irish Cream | |

1. Layer the Kahlúa and Baileys in a shot glass.
2. Float the 151 on top.
3. Ignite it.
4. Now's the time to make any hokey proclamations of undying love, which we hope will be reciprocated.
5. Extinguish by blowing out the flame.
6. Consume the shot or offer it to that special someone.

**STATS**

| SERVE IN | TECHNIQUE | POTENCY | SKILL LEVEL | DANGER |
|---|---|---|---|---|

# VESUVIUS

Orgasms have been likened to volcanic eruptions ever since Mount Vesuvius first recorded meltdown in 79 CE. Of course, not every climax actually *deserves* the comparison, but we figure 2,000 years of concerted human effort bring some legitimacy to the simile. (Just think of the accumulative huffing and puffing humping and groaning!) If you wanna throw your gauntlet into the crater, invite a willing partner to toss back a few of these with you, then do your best to get the lava flowing.

3 parts crème de cacao
1 part green Chartreuse

1 splash 151-proof rum

**1.** Layer the crème de cacao and green Chartreuse in a shot glass.

**2.** Float the 151 on top.

**3.** Ignite it. There's your volcano!

**4.** Extinguish the flame by placing an empty shot glass over the flaming one.

**5.** You are free to consume.

STATS — SERVE IN · TECHNIQUE · POTENCY · SKILL LEVEL · DANGER

# THRILL SEEKER

"I can resist everything but temptation," said Oscar Wilde, a man famous for saying many witty things he may or may not have said. If you're a thrill seeker at heart, famous for exploits you may or may not have participated in, then bottoms up: This sweet and frisky little tonic is for you—and anyone who cares to join you in your next wicked little adventure.

part strawberry liqueur
part dark rum

1. Pour the strawberry liqueur and dark rum into a shot glass neat.

2. Ignite the rum and watch it burn with a glint in your eye.

3. Thoroughly blow out the flames.

4. Shoot.

5. See what kind of trouble you can stir up next.

STATS · SERVE IN · TECHNIQUE · POTENCY · SKILL LEVEL · DANGER

# FLAMING BLUE F@*K

Moonlight, roses, and months of wistful courtship have their place (i.e. the silve screen with Audrey Hepburn as the leading lady). But we're all adults here, so let's be frank: Sometimes you just want to do it. Then do it some more. Then say you name is "Cherry Bomb" and go home without leaving so much as a piece of lin behind. When you're in one of *those* kinds of mood, this bright blue drink is you beacon: Use it to signal all the other horn dogs in the house. Ask enough people i they want a Flaming Blue F@*k, and we bet you won't go home alone.

3 parts sambuca
1 part blue curaçao

1 splash 151-proof rum

1. Pour the sambuca and blue curaçao into a shot glass neat.

2. Ignite the rum.

3. Let it burn for a few seconds.

4. Extinguish it.

5. Slam it.

6. Prepare a second one for any unattached somebody at the bar, and go from there.

STATS

Skill Level:

Serve In:        Danger:

Technique:       Potency:

# CUPID'S FLAMING ARROW

ove at first sight? Sometimes even Cupid needs a little help making things happen.
ut this drink on the evening's menu, and who knows?

| | |
|---|---|
| 1 part grenadine | ½ part ginger ale (or to taste) |
| 1 part triple sec | Lemon juice |
| 1 part vodka | 1 splash 151-proof rum |

- Fill a Collins glass with ice and add all the ingredients except for the rum.
- Float the overproof rum on top and ignite.
- Toast the memories you're about to have together, put out the flames, and drink.

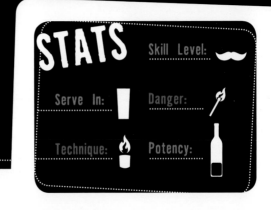

## STATS

Skill Level:

Serve In:

Danger:

Technique:

Potency:

# ALL GROWNS UP

I n the classic film *Swingers*, Trent (Vince Vaughn) proudly proclaims of best friend, Mikey, (at the top of his lungs in the Waffle House at 4 A.M.), "My baby's all growns up!" When you make the flaming shots and cocktails in this chapter, you'll be similarly proud that your drinks are all growns up. In fact, from this point onward, the drinks in this book grow more and more sophisticated.

So, the first thing you need to do is stock your bar with mature liqueurs such as anisette, sambuca, vermouth, and some fine brandy. Note: for drinks like Jerry Thomas' Blue Blazer and the Flaming Moz you'll need some patience, training, and moxie to pull them off. You may want to leave those to the professionals.

# FLAMING BLUE

Vermouth is a fortified wine aperitif, normally infused, macerated, or distilled with herbs, spices, alcohol, and a blend of other ingredients. There are two basic styles of Vermouth—French and Italian. French vermouth is generally white and quite dry. It's most famously used in the classic martini. The Italian vermouth is red and is also referred to as sweet vermouth. It's the element that takes the edge off the rye or bourbon in a traditional Manhattan cocktail. Pairing sweet vermouth with the licorice-y anisette makes for an interesting combo that will appeal to refined palettes.

1 part anisette

1 part vermouth

1 splash 151-proof rum

1. Pour the anisette and vermouth into a shot glass neat.

2. Float the 151 on top.

3. Ignite with a long match or bamboo skewer (that will look more growns up than a regular match).

4. Fully blow out the flame before you drink the shot.

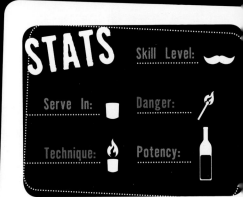

STATS

Skill Level:

Serve In:

Danger:

Technique:

Potency:

# FLAMING GIRAFFE

Pay homage to Salvador Dali's 1975 painting "The Giraffe of Avignon" with this tasty shooter. Enjoy it with your art-loving friends as a digestif after a wonderful meal or a pre-gallery-hopping aperitif.

2 parts Kahlúa
1 part butterscotch schnapps

1 part 151-proof rum

1. Pour the Kahlúa and butterscotch into a shot glass.
2. Float the 151 on top.
3. Ignite.
4. Blow out the flame with finesse before you imbibe.

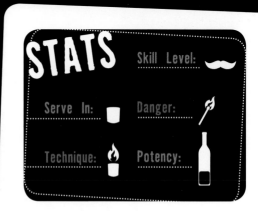

**STATS**

Skill Level:

Serve In:     Danger:

Technique:     Potency:

# FLAMING MOZ

Composing this drink requires bartending skills. It's a visual spectacle on par with a cool circus act and perfect for entertaining jaded highbrow friends who think they have seen it all. Muffy will barely be able to keep her headband in place. Take care not to spill this one on Todd's Nantucket reds.

1 part blue curaçao
1 part white sambuca

1 part green Chartreuse

1. Place a rocks glass on the bar.

2. Pour the blue curaçao, sambuca, and Chartreuse into a brandy snifter.

3. Now, here comes the circus act: Balance the snifter, horizontally, on the mouth of the rocks glass.

4. Ignite the spirits in the snifter and rotate the glass like a cement mixer on top of the rocks glass so all of the spirits are warmed.

5. While the spirits are still burning, *very carefully* pour them into the rocks glass. The stream of alcohol falling between the glasses should form a waterfall of fire cascading into th rocks glass.

6. Now that you've thoroughly impressed your audience, use the upside-down brandy snifter to suffocate the flames in the rocks glass.

7. Once you're certain the flames have gone out, remove the brandy snifter and invite a guest to inhale the fumes before shooting the contents of the glass. Now who's the mos sophisticated one of them all?

STATS | SERVE IN | TECHNIQUE | POTENCY | SKILL LEVEL | DANGER

# FLAMING GORILLA

In German, the word *schnaps* mean "mouthful," which is an apt description for the peppermint wallop delivered by this luscious shooter. Coffee and mint make good together, here. If you're wondering where the gorilla comes in, we have no idea.

1 part peppermint schnapps
1 part Kahlúa
1 part 151-proof rum

1. Layer the peppermint schnapps and then the Kahlúa in a shot glass.

2. Carefully float the 151 on top.

3. Light it up.

4. Blow it out and savor the coffee-and-mint goodness.

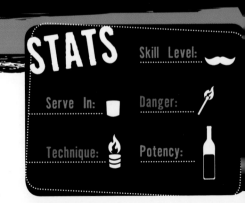

STATS

Skill Level:

Serve In:

Danger:

Technique:

Potency:

# THE CONCORDE

Back in the day, if you had the funds, you could book a flight on the Concorde and get to Paris from New York City in 3 ½ hours. What a delightful feat to celebrate. Think of speed and luxury of old as you toast to the Concorde with this sleek, smooth shooter! Do it quickly, the captain has illuminated the "No Smoking" sign!

part coffee liqueur
part Baileys Irish Cream
splash 151-proof rum

1. Layer the coffee liqueur and Baileys in a shot glass.
2. Float the 151 on top.
3. Ignite.
4. Extinguish and revel in this yummy drink and all the other joys of luxe living.

## STATS

Skill Level:

Serve In:

Danger:

Technique:

Potency:

# OUT ON THE TOWN...

# THE BRASS KNUCKLE

## (COMPLIMENTS OF GOOD LUCK, ROCHESTER, NEW YORK)

If you find yourself in Rochester, New York, seek out the restaurant Good Luck for a delightful meal or a refreshing cocktail. You won't regret it. Housed in a beautifully restored old warehouse, Good Luck has an inviting feel and a compelling look.

Chuck Cerankosky, one of Good Luck's owners, was kind enough to share one of his inventions. Like Good Luck itself, this drink is long on form and substance. It offers a double flame for thrill seekers, but also a refined spicy and sweet cocktail for discerning drinkers.

Good Luck • 50 Anderson Avenue • Rochester, NY 14607-1140 • (585) 340-6161
www.restaurantgoodluck.com

1 teaspoon raw sugar

Dash of St. George Absinthe Verte (enough to coat the glass)

1 ounce Patron Silver

1 ounce Pimms No.1

½ ounce pear nectar (without added sugar)

¼ ounce agave syrup

¼ ounce lime juice

Sriracha (the Asian chili sauce that comes in a red bottle with rooster on it)

## REPARE THE GLASS:

a coupe glass (or small margarita glass) add 1 teaspoon of raw sugar and a dash of the absinthe. irl to coat the bottom of the glass.

## REPARE THE SHAKER:

an ice-filled shaker, add the Patron, Pimms, pear, agave, lime juice and a scant 3 drops of the racha.

## HE SHOW:

ght the absinthe/sugar mixture in the glass—you'll see cool blue flames and hear faint popping as the sugar caramelizes. Quickly give the shaker approximately 30 akes and strain the liquid into the glass, extinguishing the flames. For a final show fire, hold the orange rind over top of the drink and squeeze the rind quickly near lit match ("flaming the orange"), which will make a poof of flame over the drink.

STATS

| SERVE IN | TECHNIQUE | POTENCY | SKILL LEVEL | DANGER |

# GREEN LIZARD

The not-so-secret ingredient in this pretty yellow-green shot is green Chartreuse. This aromatic liqueur gets its lizard-like color from chlorophyll, derived from the 130 herbs and spices that compose it. Known as *verte au feu* (or "green fire") in French, this exotic liqueur was designed by sixteenth-century Carthusian monks. It's still produced in Grenoble, at the foot of the French Alps, under the monastery's guidance. If you want to sound really cultured, casually mention this back story as you light your shots of rum and *verte au feu*.

4 parts green Chartreuse
1 part 151-proof rum

**1.** Pour the Chartreuse in a shot glass and float the 151 on top.

**2.** Ignite the 151.

**3.** After admiring the flames, extinguish them by placing an empty shot glass over the flaming shot.

**4.** Drink up!

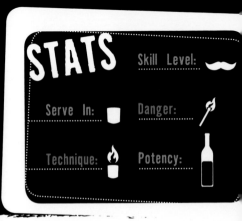

STATS

Skill Level:

Serve In:

Danger:

Technique:

Potency:

# FLAMING HENRY

This luxe tipple was created by Henry Smiff and friends in the South of Franc and popularized by one of their number, Jon Coe, the successful London drink wholesaler. It's suggested that you make this cocktail with Bulleit Bourbon although any bourbon will serve you right. Bulleit is a top-shelf, Kentucky bourbon Its honey and oaky notes pair well with the amaretto and Baileys that jointl compose this decadent drink.

1 part amaretto
1 part Baileys Irish Cream
1 part Kentucky bourbon whiskey (splurge on Bulleit if possible)

1. Carefully layer the ingredients in a shot glass in the following order: amaretto, Baileys, and bourbon.

2. Ignite the bourbon and anticipate how magnificent it's going to taste as you watch it blaze.

3. Extinguish by placing an empty shot glass over the flaming shot glass,

4. Bottoms up!

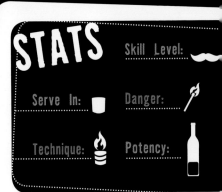

STATS

Skill Level:

Serve In:

Danger:

Technique:

Potency:

# COMBUSTIBLE EDISON

t doesn't matter if the last thing you "invented" was a space shuttle for your teddy ear when you were six, your friends will start referring to you as "the professor" fter you serve them this genius aperitif. Like many of the finer things in life, the ombustible Edison is all about presentation. While your brandy is warming in a nafing dish, you shake the Campari and lemon juice in a shaker, then strain it nto a chilled martini glass. Now, here's the part that makes you look really slick: ou light the brandy and boldly pour a fiery stream of burning booze right into the ocktail glass! We'll understand if you take a bow afterward.

1 part Campari bitters
1 part fresh lemon juice

2 parts brandy

. Combine the Campari and lemon juice in an ice-filled shaker.

. Shake and strain into a chilled cocktail glass.

. Heat the brandy in a chafing dish.

. When it's warm, ignite the brandy and *very carefully* pour the fiery stream into the cocktail glass.

. The flames will extinguish themselves.

. Serve the drink with a flourish once all flames have gone out.

STATS

| SERVE IN | TECHNIQUE | POTENCY | SKILL LEVEL | DANGER |

# FLAMING SAMBUCA

In Italy, this drink is called *sambuca con la mosca*, which translates into "sambuc with flies." The coffee beans are merely decorative, although you can chew on ther if you wish. According to tradition, you should serve this drink with exactly thre coffee beans, one for health, one for happiness, and the third for prosperity.

1-2 ounces sambuca negra
3 coffee beans

1. Place the coffee beans in a shot glass and pour in the sambuca.

2. Light the drink and let it burn for up to 10 seconds. If you have any trouble igniting th sambuca, warm the glass with hot water before you fill it. The warmth will help the spirit ignite.

3. Wet the palm of your hand with a damp rag, and quickly place it over the top of the glas to create a seal until the flames go out. Don't worry, if you do this correctly, you won't bur yourself.

4. Inhale the vapors before drinking the shot and chewing the coffee beans (or not).

## STATS

Skill Level:

Serve In:

Danger:

Technique:

Potency:

# MISSISSIPPI MUD

This tasty number will remind you of the dessert of the same name, except the buzz you get from the drink isn't from chocolate.

1 ½ ounces Southern Comfort
1 ½ ounces coffee liqueur

2 scoops vanilla ice cream
1 splash 151-proof rum

1. Place all the ingredients except for the rum in a blender and blend until smooth.

2. Pour into a cocktail glass and float the rum on top.

3. Ignite and enjoy the flames before extinguishing and enjoying this tasty concoction.

## STATS

Skill Level:

Serve In:

Danger:

Technique:

Potency:

# BLUE BLAZER

This awe-inspiring flaming drink was created at San Francisco's El Dorado Saloon by bartender Jerry Thomas, who was known as "the professor" for his inventive cocktails which are experiencing a Renaissance today. The Blue Blazer involves pouring a flaming mug of whiskey into a mug of hot water, and then back and forth, until the flames go out. Learn how to present this drink with finesse and you'll be the mixological god of every cocktail party. But be forewarned, unless you're anxious to go up in flames, the Blue Blazer should *never* be attempted by klutzes, scatterbrains, the accident prone, the sleep deprived, or those who are already inebriated. (Did we forget anyone?)

Basic instructions for this old standby are supplied below plus see page 24 for additional tips, but if you really want to master this thing—before it masters *you*—we recommend that you practice the technique with two cups of water. If you look like you wet your pants at the end of your practice section, step aside and leave this one to the pros.

--------------------------------------------------------

3 ounces boiling water      3 ounces warm blended whiskey

1 ½ teaspoons sugar or honey      1 lemon twist

--------------------------------------------------------

1. Heat two mugs (Jerry Thomas used silver tankards) by filling them with hot water and letting them stand for three minutes.

2. In one mug, combine boiling water and the sugar, stirring to dissolve.

3. Pour the warm whiskey into the other mug.

4. Ignite the whiskey with a match and, while it's blazing, *slowly* and *carefully* pour the whiskey into the hot water.

5. Again, *slowly* and *carefully*, pour the mixture back and forth from one mug to the other until the flame dies out.

6. Drop in the lemon twist and serve. Who's a hot shot?

**STATS** | SERVE IN | TECHNIQUE | POTENCY | SKILL LEVEL | DANGER

# OUT ON THE TOWN...

# CALVADOS BLAZER

## (COMPLIMENTS OF MONTGOMERY PLACE, LONDON, ENGLAND)

Montgomery Place is a classic American cocktail bar, a throwback to the Rat Pack days when cocktails were king and even a ten-year-old could make a proper martini for daddy. Revered for consistently producing quality cocktails, a visit to Montgomery Place is a must do when you find yourself across the pond.

Here they have modified a drink called the "Blazer," but the talented mixologist Agostino Perrone recommends that you further customize the drink by using your guest's favorite spirits and playing with the selection of spices and fruits. The drink is blazed only for a short time—generally a few seconds so it doesn't alter the alcohol much—but long enough to heat the whole contents of the drink, so the flavors blend and the sugar has a chance to caramelize. This drink is best enjoyed on very cold days. It's strong and flavorful—a fast way to warm up. In fact, one should be enough.

Montgomery Place • 31 Kensington Park Road • Notting Hill, London • Telephone: +44 20 7792 3921
www.montgomeryplace.co.uk

1 ½ ounces Calvados brandy

¼ ounce maple syrup

1 dash Velvet Falernum

1 dash Angostura bitters

1 fresh raspberry

2 to 3 coffee beans

Small stick of cinnamon

1 to 2 cloves

2 to 3 small strips lemongrass

Small twists orange and lemon

## PREPARE THE DRINK:

nd a glass that will sit perfectly on a double rocks glass (wine or brandy balloon). Have
 serving glass at the ready. Pour hot water into the rocks glass so it touches and heats
e sitting glass. Put all the ingredients into a wine glass and let the spirits warm up (1-2
inutes). Set it on fire and swirl the glass gently. *Work fast* so the glass doesn't break. Let
e fire burn for 10 to 15 seconds at most. Pour the contents into a serving glass from a height
 1 foot or so—this will ensure it mixes in the serving glass as well. *Work carefully* so the
urning alcohol goes into serving glass only.

## XTINGUISH THE FLAMES:

ll the fire by covering the rim of the serving glass with a small plate or glass of a similar size.

## OW TO DRINK IT:

eathe the alcohol vapors in first, hold your breath, then take a sip. Now release the air.
llow this sequence each time you drink so you enjoy the aroma as well as the flavor of this
ink.

**STATS**

| SERVE IN | TECHNIQUE | POTENCY | SKILL LEVEL | DANGER |

# DEATH FROM ABOVE

Like mortgage payments, taxes, and the horrifying realization that your belly/breasts/earlobes are gradually succumbing to gravity, death is one of those distasteful things we all must reckon with. Philosophical sorts play mind games to try to make sense of the inevitable, while religious types turn their fears over to a higher power. And then there's the rest of us. When faced with the reality of death, we drink. This particular concoction takes some setup time, which makes it the perfect choice to take your mind off little worries—like when and how you'll die—that might otherwise preoccupy you. Silly you!

1 part gin
1 part 151-proof rum

3 parts cola

1. Put some rocks glasses in your freezer to chill.

2. When they're freezing to the touch, remove them from the freezer.

3. Pour in the gin and then the 151, leaving enough room in the glass for cola.

4. Light the mixture on fire for a few dazzling seconds.

5. Add the cola. Once the cola has fully extinguished the flames, drink up!

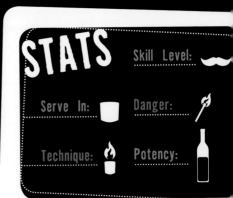

STATS

Skill Level:

Serve In:

Danger:

Technique:

Potency:

# MOLOTOV COCKTAIL

Whoa! Don't get the wrong idea here. We're not going to teach you how to make bombs from common household items. The Molotov Cocktail we have in mind is very civilized—in fact, it may be a bit of a sissy. It features the venerable Chartreuse—an herbal liqueur made by peace-loving monks—and a rather innocuous ruby port which together create pretty green and red layers in your shot glass. After you set it alight and blow it out, you and your pals can go back to chatting about all sorts of revolutionary news, such as your dreadful peanut allergy and your friend's morbid fear of spiders.

2 parts green Chartreuse
1 part ruby port

1. Pour the Chartreuse in a shot glass and float the port on top
2. Ignite the port.
3. Enjoy a few seconds of fame and flame.
4. Thoroughly blow out the flames before drinking.

## STATS

Skill Level:

Serve In:

Danger:

Technique:

Potency:

# STOCK MARKET CRASH

fter years of looking forward to that day when you can leave the confines of your parent's home and make your own fortune, that day has finally arrived. You have the ot job, hot car, hot lover, and hot stocks. You're on top of the world—who knows, maybe you'll cash in your chips early and retire at forty? Or how about inviting that weet someone over to roll around with you in a sea of money? But lo and behold, here's actually something more powerful than your ego. It's a universal law of e marketplace, and it goes something like this: What goes up must come down. When you come face to face with this sobering reality, here's the perfect recipe to rown your sorrows. It's easy to mix and even easier to drink. (Plus, lighting s#*t n fire always helps when you're feeling like a moron.)

1 ounce Goldschläger
1 ounce 151-proof rum

8 ounces cola

. Pour the Goldschläger into a shot glass and float the 151 on top.

. Pour the cola into a beer mug; it should be full enough to extinguish the flames when you dunk the shot glass.

. Ignite the contents of the shot glass and then *quickly and carefully, before it gets too hot*, drop the shot glass into the glass filled with cola.

. When the flames are completely extinguished, you can chug!

STATS | SERVE IN | TECHNIQUE | POTENCY | SKILL LEVEL | DANGER

# THE SUNSET

Just as a beautiful sunset announces the end of the day, this lovely-to-look-at shot should announce the end of a dinner party . . . and the beginning of the after-dinner party festivities.

1 part grenadine
1 part coffee liqueur
1 part Baileys Irish Cream
1 part crème de banana
1 part 151-proof rum

1. Layer in a shot glass in this order: grenadine, coffee liqueur, Baileys, and crème de banana.

2. Float the 151 on top and ignite it.

3. Admire your sunset before extinguishing the flame with an empty shot glass.

## STATS

Skill Level:

Serve In:

Danger:

Technique:

Potency:

# CHOCOLATE-
# COVERED CHERRY

his dessert shot tastes like dark chocolate and goes great with a cup of java. It's
lso a treat for the eyes as the cherry is suspended in the middle of the drink. This
rink is better sipped than slammed since you don't want to choke on the cherry!

laraschino cherry
part grenadine
part Kahlúa
part Baileys Irish Cream
part 151-proof rum

**1.** Remove the stem from the cherry and drop the cherry
in the shot glass.

**2.** Layer the grenadine, Kahlúa, and Baileys in the shot
glass.

**3.** Float the 151 on top and ignite it. Blow out the flame
before drinking.

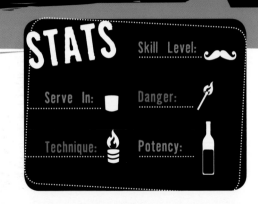

# STATS

Skill Level:

Serve In:     Danger:

Technique:    Potency:

# FLAMING SEVEN & SEVEN

Here's a flaming version of the popular highball—for when you want to feel grow up, but aren't quite ready to don the Bermuda shorts with the black socks.

2 ounces Seagram's 7 Crown whiskey
12 ounces lemon-lime soda

1. Pour the whiskey into a double shot glass.

2. Pour the soda in a Collins glass.

3. Warm the shot glass by immersing it in a bowl of hot water.

4. Light the whiskey and then drop it into the soda.

5. Make sure all the flames have gone out, stir, and commence conversing about matur things like taxes and life insurance.

**STATS**

Skill Level:

Serve In:   Danger:

Technique:   Potency:

# FLAMING ARMADILLO

Feeling like you need to get out of your armored shell and let loose? Often accused of burrowing when you should be socializing? Have a couple of these little critters and you'll be all set.

1 part amaretto almond liqueur     1 splash 151-proof rum
1 part tequila

1. Pour the amaretto and tequila into a shot glass.
2. Float the overproof rum on top.
3. Light the drink and admire it before extinguishing the flames. Consume.

STATS

Skill Level:

Serve In:     Danger:

Technique:     Potency:

# FLAMING HOT DRINKS TO HEAL WHAT "ALES" YOU

**H**ere you'll find flaming coffees, grogs, ciders, and two delicious versions of a punch called the English Bishop. Many of the drinks in this chapter are centuries old and call for clove-studded baked oranges, cinnamon ticks, and generous helpings of cognac. You'll feel like you've stepped ack in time to a kinder, gentler era when many used alcohol primarily for medicinal (as opposed to entertainment) purposes. We can't guarantee it, but hese drinks may have some healing powers.

Perfect for winter celebrations, ski weekends, snow days . . . Few things ay "I love you" better than the spicy and aromatic smells that will waft hrough your house as you prepare the recipes found herein. Light a fire, vite your dear friends and family to cozy up, and enjoy!

# FLAMING HOT BUTTERED RUM

A steaming mug of hot buttered rum conjures up all sorts of cozy images. You i
a warm flannel shirt and slippers, curled up in a big leather armchair in front of a
cheerful fire, your faithful golden retriever at your feet. Now, let's strike a match
and light up some mugs of rum and a different picture emerges. We see you and al
your friends, partying in a ski lodge after a long day on the slopes. This flaming ho
potion leads to a smoking hot time in the hot tub. Ooh la la!

| | |
|---|---|
| 1 tablespoon brown sugar | 2 to 3 ounces dark Jamaican rum |
| Cinnamon stick | 1 pinch sugar |
| 1 small slice lemon peel | ½ ounce 151-proof rum |
| Whole cloves to taste | Pat of butter |
| Boiling water | |

**1.** Warm a large, heatproof Irish coffee mug by rinsing it out with boiling water.

**2.** Add the brown sugar, cinnamon stick, and lemon peel studded with cloves.

**3.** Pour in enough boiling water to dissolve the sugar and then stir in the dark Jamaican rum

**4.** Fill the mug with boiling water.

**5.** Warm the 151 and a pinch of sugar in a ladle or spoon by partially immersing the bowl c
the ladle in hot water.

**6.** Ignite the 151 and *very carefully* pour the still blazing rum into the mug.

**7.** Stir rapidly until the flames are fully extinguished, then top with the pat of butter and serve ho

## STATS

| SERVE IN | TECHNIQUE | POTENCY | SKILL LEVEL | DANGER |
|---|---|---|---|---|
|  |  |  |  |  |

# THE BLACK STRIPE

Want to take away the winter doldrums? Invite over a bunch of friends who have nothing better to do, fill some mugs with this blazing hot drink, and let the good times roll. Some molasses dissolved in hot water is your black stripe. Lemon peel, cinnamon sticks, and more hot water follow. The fun part comes when you ignite some Jamaican rum on the top. That and a sprinkling of nutmeg will make it feel like Christmas.

| | |
|---|---|
| 2 teaspoons molasses | Cinnamon stick |
| Boiling water | 2 to 3 ounces dark Jamaican rum |
| Lemon peel | 1 pinch freshly grated nutmeg |

**1.** In a heatproof beer mug dissolve molasses with a little boiling water.

**2.** Add lemon peel, cinnamon stick, and more boiling water.

**3.** Float the rum on top.

**4.** Ignite and let it blaze briefly before stirring rapidly to extinguish the flames.

**5.** Top with a sprinkling of nutmeg and serve hot.

STATS | SERVE IN | TECHNIQUE | POTENCY | SKILL LEVEL | DANGER

# JERSEY FLASH

Jersey is known for many things: sulfur smells, turnpikes, Tony Soprano, and now the fist-pumping cast of the train wreck show, *The Jersey Shore.*

There is a kinder, more genteel Jersey, one where Jackie O boarded her horses and where sprawling apple orchards were in abundance. Though not as plentiful as in the 1800s when two-thirds of the state was covered with apple trees and apple cider was one of the state's leading exports, New Jersey still makes some apple cider worth sampling in this drink.

After a brisk day in the pumpkin patch, bring the kiddies home for some cider and molasses cookies. You can make this adults-only hot cider for you and your friends. It'll take the edge off your screaming kids.

| | |
|---|---|
| 1 teaspoon honey | Boiling water |
| 4 whole cloves | 2 ounces gin |
| 1 pinch cinnamon | Hot apple cider |
| 1 small lemon peel | 1 pinch freshly grated nutmeg |

1. Rinse out a heatproof Irish coffee mug with boiling water to warm it.
2. Add the honey, cloves, cinnamon, lemon peel, and a little boiling water to dissolve the honey.
3. Warm the gin by rinsing a shot glass out with boiling water, then adding the gin.
4. Add the warmed gin to the coffee mug.
5. Ignite it and let it blaze for a few seconds.
6. Fill the mug with hot cider, stirring rapidly to extinguish the flames.
7. Sprinkle with grated nutmeg and serve hot.

**STATS**

| SERVE IN | TECHNIQUE | POTENCY | SKILL LEVEL | DANGER |
|---|---|---|---|---|

# ABERDEEN ANGUS

Aberdeen Angus are black, hornless cattle. Originally bred in Scotland, today it's a preferred breed for beef in the U.S. What does this have to do with a flaming hot drink? We don't have the foggiest idea. What we can tell you is that this warming whiskey drink is an unbeatable choice for taking the chill off on a cold winter's evening. You can use any Scotch whiskey, but for authenticity's sake, pick up some Drambuie, which is sweetened with heather honey. Serve it to friends around a great roaring fire. If you share enough rounds, they may overlook the phony Scottish brogue you've adopted for the night.

2 ounces Scotch whiskey      1 tablespoon honey

1 ounce Drambuie      2 tablespoons lime juice

**1.** Warm an Irish coffee mug by rinsing it in boiling water.

**2.** Pour the Scotch whiskey, honey, and lime juice in the mug and stir.

**3.** Warm the Drambuie in a ladle by partially immersing the ladle in hot water.

**4.** Ignite it, then *very carefully* pour the still burning scotch into the mug.

**5.** Stir rapidly until the flames are fully extinguished, then serve hot.

 STATS

| SERVE IN | TECHNIQUE | POTENCY | SKILL LEVEL | DANGER |
|----------|-----------|---------|-------------|--------|
|  |  |  |  |  |

# CAFÉ DIABLO

Cointreau and cognac are the signature alcohols in this most famous of flaming coffee drinks. While this duo burbles in a pan that includes orange and sometimes lemon peel and always a clove or two, you fill mugs with piping hot coffee. When it's time to serve, ignite the alcohol and pour it, still blazing, into the mugs of coffee. Your guests will be entranced by your extreme-bartending prowess. But remember, a presentation like this takes practice: Try it a few times without an audience first. (Trust us: Burning yourself in front of your guests would put a damper on your party.)

---

1 ounce cognac

½ ounce Cointreau

1 to 2 whole cloves

1 long strip of lemon peel

1 long strip of orange peel

6 ounces hot strong black coffee

1 cinnamon stick for garnish (optional)

---

**1.** In a saucepan over medium heat, combine the cognac, Cointreau, cloves, and citrus peel, stirring often.

**2.** Pour the hot coffee into a heat-resistant mug, and set aside.

**3.** As bubbles form around the edge of the pan, use a long match to ignite the alcohol.

**4.** *Quickly and carefully* pour the flaming alcohol into the mug of hot coffee.

**5.** After the coffee fully extinguishes the flame, you are free to drink.

**6.** Garnish with a cinnamon stick if desired.

STATS    SERVE IN    TECHNIQUE    POTENCY    SKILL LEVEL    DANGER

# ENGLISH BISHOP

Ahh, the warm, inviting smell of clove-studded baked oranges and simmered cinnamon sticks. Here you'll find a classic punch recipe that will instantly make your guests feel welcome.

There's something Dickensian and Christmas-y about a bowl of this aromatic flaming punch. Let it transport you and your guests to nineteenth-century England. Serve with a smile, and there's a good chance they could turn your Scrooges into Fezziwigs before the night is through!

| | |
|---|---|
| 5 large oranges | One 750 ml bottle dark Jamaican rum |
| Brown sugar | ½ gallon apple cider |
| Whole cloves | Freshly grated nutmeg for garnish |
| 3 to 4 cinnamon sticks | |

1. Dampen the outside of the oranges with a moist paper towel, then coat them with brown sugar and stud each orange with a dozen cloves.

2. Arrange them in a roasting pan and thoroughly brown them in a 350°F broiler until juice begins to seep out of the oranges.

3. Quarter the oranges and place them in a heatproof punch bowl.

4. Add the cinnamon sticks and sprinkle a little more brown sugar on the oranges to soak up the juices.

5. Warm the apple cider in a pot on the stovetop.

6. Warm the rum over low heat in the top of a chafing dish, then pour it into the punch bowl.

7. Ignite it, and let it blaze for a few seconds.

8. Extinguish the flames by adding the hot apple cider to the punch bowl and stirring rapidly.

9. Serve hot in punch cups topped with a sprinkling of nutmeg. Makes 24 servings.

STATS — SERVE IN — TECHNIQUE — POTENCY — SKILL LEVEL — DANGER

# ROMAN COFFEE

This delectable coffee drink employs flaming Galliano, a sweet syrupy Italian liqueur, to caramelize sugar in mugs before you fill them with coffee, whipped cream, and a sprinkling of cinnamon and nutmeg. This is the perfect after-dinner drink—or stand-in for dessert—to serve to a special date, your in-laws, or even your boss. To dress it up, consider using thin crystal tulip glasses; just be sure to continually rotate the glasses for even heating while you caramelize the sugar. (Otherwise, you risk shattering the glass!)

1 wedge lemon

2 teaspoons sugar

1 ounce Galliano herbal liqueur

Hot, strong black coffee

1 pinch cinnamon

1 pinch freshly grated nutmeg

Dollop of whipped cream

1. Squeeze a lemon wedge inside an Irish coffee mug, then use the wedge to wipe the juice all around the inside of the mug.

2. Empty excess juice.

3. Next add the sugar and rotate the mug until the sugar completely covers the inside of the glass.

4. Rinse a shot glass with boiling water, then pour in the Galliano.

5. Add the warmed Galliano to the mug and ignite it, rotating the glass to avoid uneven heating, until the sugar is caramelized.

6. Add the coffee, which will extinguish the flame.

7. Top it off with whipped cream and sprinkle with the cinnamon and nutmeg.

8. Serve immediately.

STATS

| SERVE IN | TECHNIQUE | POTENCY | SKILL LEVEL | DANGER |

# CAFÉ BRÛLOT

Celebrate the Roaring Twenties with a prohibition party that features this splendid drink. According to a legend we choose to believe, this was the perfect prohibition punch because the coffee aroma helped disguise the boozy smell of the cognac. You'll need a big punch bowl, warmed coffee mugs, and a lighter. And it wouldn't hurt if you and your main squeeze dressed yourselves like Zelda and F. Scott or some other members of the Lost Generation.

4 parts cognac

1 part white curaçao

16 parts hot strong black coffee

2 cinnamon sticks

12 whole cloves

Peels of 2 lemons and 2 oranges cut into twists

4 sugar cubes

1. In a large, heatproof punch bowl, mash together the cinnamon sticks, cloves, fruit peels, and sugar cubes, softening the sugar cubes with a little water if necessary.

2. Stir in the cognac and curaçao.

3. Ignite and then gradually add the hot coffee, stirring gently until the flames are completely extinguished.

4. Ladle into warmed mugs.

STATS

| SERVE IN | TECHNIQUE | POTENCY | SKILL LEVEL | DANGER |

# ALHAMBRA ROYALE

This classic, thoroughly grown-up hot chocolate drink will be a hit with every chocolate lover you know. However, the technique requires more than a little finesse: You must warm cognac in a ladle before igniting and pouring it into mugs—all while you continue with an uninterrupted stream of cocktail party chatter. So be sure to practice a few times before you attempt to present this delectable treat as the grand finale of your next dinner party.

| | |
|---|---|
| 1 cup hot chocolate | 1 ½ ounces cognac |
| 1 wide slice orange peel | Dollop of whipped cream (optional) |

**1.** Fill Irish coffee mug two-thirds full with hot chocolate.

**2.** Twist the orange peel over the mug to release essential oils, then drop it in.

**3.** Warm the cognac in a ladle by partially immersing it in hot water.

**4.** Ignite, and then pour *very carefully* the still flaming cognac into the mug.

**5.** Stir rapidly to extinguish the flame.

**6.** Top with a dollop of whipped cream, if you wish.

| SERVE IN | TECHNIQUE | POTENCY | SKILL LEVEL | DANGER |
|---|---|---|---|---|
|  |  |  |  |  |

STATS

# CAFÉ NAPOLEON

Curl up by the fire with some friends and watch the snowflakes fall while drinking this decadent flaming coffee drink. It's the perfect remedy for post-snowball-fight soreness. Yes, you will need a well-stocked bar and pantry to pull this one off, but although there are many ingredients, if you follow the instructions precisely, you can produce this classic hot drink.

Note: You may be wondering what kümmel and B&B liqueur are. Kümmel means "caraway seed" in German. This German liqueur is infused with caraway, cumin, and various other herbs. Meanwhile, in the 1930s, a Manhattan bartender combined Benedictine and fine French brandy creating Benedictine and Brandy. As the company says on their website, "The drink was an instant classic, the name was shortened, and the rest is history." (Benedictine, made of herbs, roots and sugar with a cognac base, has a rich history dating back to 1510. Those boozehound monks created it, and they reportedly used it to revive their tired souls. Amen, brothers!)

| | | |
|---|---|---|
| 2 tablespoons honey | 8 whole cloves | 1 ounce gold rum |
| Zest of ½ orange | 4 cups hot, strong black coffee | 1 ounce cognac |
| 1 teaspoon lemon juice | 2 ounces B&B liqueur | Whipped cream for topping |
| 2 to 3 cinnamon sticks | 1 ounce kümmel | Freshly grated nutmeg for garnish |

1. Combine the honey, orange zest, lemon juice, cinnamon sticks, cloves, and coffee in the flaming pan of a chafing dish over direct heat.

2. Bring to a simmer, but do not boil.

3. Add the B&B, kümmel, and rum; stir well.

4. Warm the cognac in a ladle by partially immersing the bowl of the ladle in hot water

5. Ignite it.

6. *Very carefully* pour the still blazing cognac into the chafing dish.

7. Stir until the flames are fully extinguished.

8. Serve in Irish coffee mugs topped with whipped cream and a sprinkling of nutmeg. Makes 4 servings.

STATS — SERVE IN · TECHNIQUE · POTENCY · SKILL LEVEL · DANGER

# CAFÉ ROYALE

Simple and elegant, this drink warms the heart and soul. It's the perfect accompaniment to a hearty meal after a long day on the slopes. Traditional Café Royale is nice. Café Royale with flambéed brandy is divine. The candied sugar cube created by the fiery brandy adds depth of flavor and gives it a nice kick.

1 cup hot, strong, black coffee
1 sugar cube

½ ounce brandy
1 tablespoon heavy cream

. Warm a heatproof Irish coffee mug by rinsing it out with boiling water.

. Pour the hot coffee into the warmed mug.

. Soak the sugar cube with the brandy in a spoon.

. Place the spoon over the mug, resting it on the rim over the coffee.

. *Very carefully* ignite the brandy-soaked sugar cube.

. Once the flame has burned out, stir the brandied sugar into the coffee.

  Float the cream on top and serve hot.

| SERVE IN | TECHNIQUE | POTENCY | SKILL LEVEL | DANGER |
|----------|-----------|---------|-------------|--------|
|  |  |  |  |  |

# COFFEE GROG

Elaborate, but worth the effort. Looks decadent. Tastes like Christmas. Make it fo
comrades you really love.

1 teaspoon butter
1 tablespoon brown sugar
Freshly grated nutmeg
12 whole cloves
4 cinnamon sticks
4 small slices lemon peel
4 small slices orange peel
1 cup dark Jamaican rum
Hot, strong black coffee
Whipped cream (optional)

1. Cream butter with brown sugar and several pinche
   of nutmeg.

2. Divide this mixture between 4 heatproof mugs.

3. Add the following to each mug: 3 cloves, a cinnamo
   stick, a slice of lemon peel, a slice of orange pee
   and 2 ounces rum (see Tip).

4. Ignite the rum and allow it to blaze for a fe
   seconds.

5. Pour in the coffee, stirring rapidly to combine th
   ingredients and extinguish the flames.

6. Top with a dollop of whipped cream if you wis
   Makes four servings.

Warming the rum in advance will make
it easier to ignite. Simply rinse a shot
glass with boiling water, then add the
rum to warm it.

STATS

Skill Level:

Serve In:    Danger:

Technique:    Potency:

# HOT VESUVIO

Mount Vesuvius (Monte Vesuvio in Italiano) is a powerful volcano that famously erupted in 79 CE killing thousands in Pompeii and Herculaneum. At the time these places served as getaway destinations for wealthy Romans much like the Hamptons serve as a delicious escape for New York's upper crust.

Celebrate decadence with your friends by serving this tummy-warming coffee. The flamed sambuca caramelizes the sugar, which adds delightful sweetness. The sugar sometimes sparks, creating a pyrotechnic display that can amaze, but take care it does not set things ablaze. Take it from the Pompeians, running from a fiery mass is a tremendous buzz kill.

---

1 cup hot strong black coffee          1 sugar cube

1 ounce sambuca

---

1. Warm an Irish coffee mug by rinsing it out with boiling water.

2. Fill the mug with hot coffee and, using an inverted teaspoon, carefully float half of the sambuca on top of the coffee.

3. Place a sugar cube in a spoon and pour the remainder of the sambuca into the spoon.

4. Ignite and dip the blazing spoon into the cup.

5. Let the cup flame for a few seconds and stir the coffee to extinguish the flames.

STATS

Skill Level:

Serve In:          Danger:

Technique:          Potency:

# MORE QUAFFABLE QUOTATIONS

What's drinking?
A mere pause from thinking!
–Lord Byron

If you drink, don't drive. Don't even putt.
–Dean Martin

I like to drink martinis
Two at the very most.
Three, I'm under the table;
Four, I'm under my host.
–Dorothy Parker

No poems can please for long or live that are written by water-drinkers.
–Horace

There can't be good living where there is not good drinking.
–Benjamin Franklin

When men drink, then they are rich and successful and win lawsuits and are happy and help their friends. Quickly, bring me a beaker of wine, so that I may wet my mind and say something clever.
–Aristophanes

There is nothing wrong with sobriety in moderation.
–John Ciardi

(Drink) . . . it provokes the desire, but it takes away the performance ....
–William Shakespeare

Sometimes too much to drink is barely enough. –Mark Twain

# BLAZING PUNCHES FOR FESTIVE FROLICS

**Y**ou'll find punches and cocktails in this chapter to help you celebrate the season with those closest to you. Keep this handy during the winter months when you want to step back in time and delight your brood with a variety of traditional holiday punches (see note). Renowned Boston bartender Josey Packard shares her recipe and unique technique for making one of these classic punches. It comes complete with instructions for a pyrotechnic display that will make your party the talk around the water cooler on Monday. Keeping up with Joneses was never so inexpensive!

There are also some drinks that pay homage to the sweet tooths in our bunch. The Flaming Chocolate Orange, Hot Apple Pie, and Pumpkin Pie in a Glass are perfect ways to sweeten up a party or cap an intimate holiday dinner. Enjoy!

Note: We don't want to put a damper on the holiday joy, but please be *extremely careful* when igniting any of the punch recipes. You should have a lid as big as your pan or punch bowl and a household fire extinguisher handy whenever you are dealing with such a large quantity of flaming alcohol. If the alcohol is flamed in a punch bowl, be sure to use a heatproof bowl and quickly extinguish the flames to avoid the possibility of the bowl shattering. Now, back to your regular holiday programming....

# HOT APPLE PIE

If you prefer apple pie to pumpkin, then try a "slice" of this. The Baileys lends this drinkable dessert a creamy à la mode flavor. Some also refer to this shot as "Baileys Comet" because the cinnamon creates a magical trail of sparkles reminiscent of the famous Halley's Comet (only you don't have to wait 75 years to see this light show!

1 part Baileys Irish Cream

1 part Goldschläger

1 splash 151-proof rum

1 dash cinnamon

1. Layer the Baileys and the Goldschlägers in a shot glass.

2. Carefully float the 151 on top.

3. Ignite it.

4. Sprinkle the cinnamon on top and enjoy the trail of sparks it creates—along with the warm apple pie smell that develops.

5. Extinguish the flames by placing an empty shot glass over the flaming one, then indulge in your liquid slice of pie.

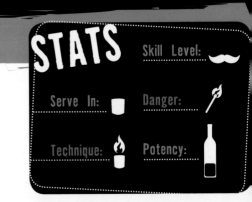

**STATS**

Skill Level:

Serve In:

Danger:

Technique:

Potency:

# FLAMING ZOMBIE

There are many ways you can create a Flaming Zombie, but we decided to go with the one with the most bang for its buck. (You don't call something a "Zombie" unless it's going to leave you lurching sideways, right?!) Remove some of the rum if you prefer more fruit and less zombification.

1 part light rum
1 part dark rum
1 part gold rum
1 part apricot brandy
½ part lime juice
½ part lemon juice

1-2 parts orange juice
1-2 parts pineapple juice
¼ part 151-proof rum
Orange slices
Maraschino cherries

1. Combine all the ingredients except for the overproof rum in a heatproof punch bowl. Feel free to experiment with other tropical juices if you wish!

2. Mix thoroughly and adjust ingredients to taste. Garnish with orange slices and maraschino cherries.

3. Float the 151 on top and ignite it (it may take a moment or two).

4. Extinguish the flames, pour, and wait for your party's inner zombie to reveal itself.

STATS — SERVE IN — TECHNIQUE — POTENCY — SKILL LEVEL — DANGER

# FLAMING GLACIER

This cinnamon- and peppermint-flavored shot is as festive as it is refreshing.

1 part cinnamon schnapps
1 part peppermint schnapps
1 splash 151-proof rum

**1.** Pour the cinnamon and peppermint schnapps into shot glass neat.

**2.** Float the 151 on top

**3.** Ignite it, and let your Flaming Glacier blaze for few seconds.

**4.** To extinguish, place an empty shot glass over th flaming shot, then it's bottom's up!

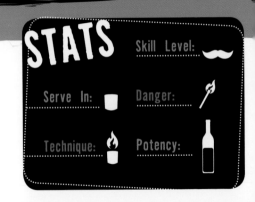

## STATS

Serve In:

Technique:

Skill Level:

Danger:

Potency:

# GLÖGG

If you want to evoke images of sugarplums dancing in your friends' heads, invite them over for a popular Scandinavian tradition, a glögg party. The word glögg (pronounced "gloog," believe it or not) derives from the Swedish verb *glodga*, meaning to burn or mull. In this case, when you *glodga* your wine with cardamom seeds, cinnamon, citrus, almonds, raisins, and cloves, your house will smell of Christmas.

Many glögg aficionados advise you to age your glögg a day or two and reheat it for your guests. The flavors have time to marry and steep, so the glögg goes from very good to transcendent. We've included a recipe that's both enticing and traditional, but there are many variations of glögg; some use vodka instead of brandy, while others incorporate orange peel, fennel seeds, or dried figs into the mix.

12 ounces brandy

One 375 ml bottle dry red wine

8 whole cloves

3 cardamom pods, crushed

1 cinnamon stick

½ cup raisins

½ cup blanched almonds

¾ cup granulated sugar

2 teaspoons brown sugar

1. In a large saucepan, combine the brandy, wine, cloves, crushed cardamom pods, cinnamon stick, raisins, almonds, and granulated sugar.

2. Set over medium-high heat and stir frequently until the sugar dissolves.

3. Just before the mixture boils, *very carefully* ignite it by touching a burning match to the surface.

4. Sprinkle the brown sugar onto the flames.

5. After 10 seconds, extinguish the flames by covering the pan with its lid.

6. To serve, spoon some raisins and almonds out of the mixture into Irish coffee mugs before adding the glögg. Makes 8 servings.

STATS | SERVE IN | TECHNIQUE | POTENCY | SKILL LEVEL | DANGER

# OLD OXFORD UNIVERSITY HOT RUM PUNCH

You don't have to be affiliated with this formidable academic institution to enjoy a cup of this hot rum punch. Versions of this classic appeared in Charles Baker's *Gentleman's Companion* (1946) and Jerry Thomas's *How to Mix Drinks* (1887), so why not go old school and serve this winter warmer at your next holiday party?

| | |
|---|---|
| 1 cup brown sugar | One 750 ml bottle 151-proof Demerara rum |
| 2 quarts boiling water | Cinnamon sticks for garnish |
| 2 cups lemon juice | Spiral of lemon peel for garnish |
| One 750 ml bottle cognac | |

1. Add the brown sugar and the boiling water to the flaming pan of a chafing dish, stirring until the sugar is dissolved.
2. Add the lemon juice and cognac. Heat but do not boil.
3. Pour in the rum, reserving several ounces for flaming.
4. Warm the reserved rum in a long-handled ladle.
5. Ignite it, and pour the still blazing rum into the chafing dish.
6. After a few seconds, extinguish the flames with the pan's lid.
7. Garnish with cinnamon sticks and lemon peel and serve hot.

STATS — SERVE IN   TECHNIQUE   POTENCY   SKILL LEVEL   DANGER

# OUT ON THE TOWN...

# EL MOROCCAN BLAZER

## (COMPLIMENTS OF DER RAUM, MELBOURNE, AUSTRALIA)

Our friends from Down Under at the highly acclaimed cocktail bar Der Raum, in Melbourne, Australia, have kindly offered this next fetching libation.

*Jigger, Beaker & Glass* by the late, great Charles H. Banker is revered in cocktail circles, not only because it provides classic recipes but also for its compelling anecdotes about the drinks' origins. This recipe caught the attention of Der Raum's owner, Matthew Bax, and served as the inspiration for the El Moroccan Blazer.

Der Raum • 438 Church Street Richmond, Melbourne • Telephone: 00 613 9428 0055
www.derraum.com/au

.............................................................................................

1 ounce cognac
½ ounce port
½ ounce Cointreau
1 teaspoon pomegranate molasses

2 teaspoons brown sugar
3 slices pineapple
2 wedges lime

## CARAMELIZE THE FRUIT:

While preparing the fruit, chill a large stemless brandy glass with crushed ice. In a frying pan, cover the fruit wedges with brown sugar and scorch with a kitchen blowtorch for approximately minute, until sugar has caramelized.

## SHAKE AND DOUBLE STRAIN:

Add contents of the frying pan to a cocktail shaker, then shake to release the juice and oils from the fruit. Add all the other ingredients and shake with the crushed ice. Remove the crushed ice from the glass and fill with blocked ice; double strain into a glass. (Due to the fruit and brown sugar, double straining is essential.) Garnish with dehydrated pineapple. (Thin slices of pineapple can be dehydrated at a low temperature in the oven. Der Raum coats theirs in Angostura Bitters beforehand, which adds a lovely spice that complements the drink's flavor profile.)

## NOTE:

If this drink sounds like a lot of work (and you don't own a chef's blowtorch), visit the masters at Der Raum in Melbourne and let them make it for you. And take a drive along Great Ocean Road to see the Twelve Apostles before they fall into the ocean. Bon voyage!

**STATS**

| SERVE IN | TECHNIQUE | POTENCY | SKILL LEVEL | DANGER |

# FLAMING HOT CHOCOLATE

You may not be a kid anymore, but surely you still yearn for a cup of hot chocolate after holiday shopping, ice skating, snow shoveling, or cookie making. Here's a version that's as grown up as you are.

3 parts dark crème de cacao
1 part 151-proof rum

**1.** Pour the crème de cacao in a shot glass.

**2.** Float the 151 on top.

**3.** Ignite it.

**4.** Let it blaze until your hot chocolate is truly hot (5 to 10 seconds).

**5.** Thoroughly blow out the flame and sip your shot.

STATS

Skill Level:

Serve In:

Danger:

Technique:

Potency:

# FLAMING
# CHOCOLATE ORANGE

Every chocolate lover knows that chocolate plus orange equals scrumptious. Here we combine the two in a festive drink that's perfect for a holiday housewarming party or as a treat to welcome unexpected guests.

3 parts Baileys Irish Cream
1 part Cointreau

1. Layer the Baileys and then the Cointreau in a shot glass.

2. Ignite the Cointreau and let it burn for a few seconds so the chocolate and orange flavors have a chance to mingle.

3. Extinguish by placing an empty shot glass over then flaming shot glass.

4. Sip this dessert in a shot glass.

**STATS**

Skill Level:

Serve In:     Danger:

Technique:     Potency:

# PUMPKIN PIE IN A GLASS

This pretty, layered shot is fun to do around the holidays. If your lovely relatives grate on you a bit after several hours of exposure, fire up some of these shooters to enjoy with your cousins. It'll definitely liven up that game of Balderdash!

1 part Kahlúa
1 part Baileys Irish Cream
1 part tequila blanco
1 dash cinnamon

1. Carefully layer the ingredients in a shot glass in the following order: Kahlúa, Baileys, and then the tequila on top.

2. Light the tequila on fire.

3. Sprinkle the cinnamon on the flames and see it sparkle.

4. Blow out the flames and enjoy your dessert . . . Yum, just like Grandma's warm pumpkin pie!

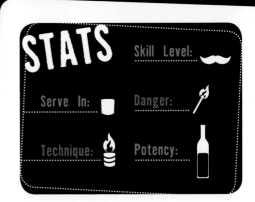

**STATS**

Skill Level:

Serve In:

Danger:

Technique:

Potency:

# KRAMBAMBULA PUNCH

Krambambula is many things: a deep red spirit, a dog in a centuries-old story about menacing gypsies, and the subject of a fraternity hymn. Here it's a lovely punch that will offer some nice fruit and sweet notes, but also a depth of flavor from the flambéed elements. Swedish punsch, a spicy-sweet rum-based liqueur, is the secret ingredient in this version.

Fire up the stove and get ready to impress your guests!

Two 750 ml bottles dry red wine
Juice of 2 oranges
Juice of 2 lemons

1 cup superfine sugar
1 pint dark Jamaican rum
1 pint Swedish punsch

1. Pour the wine and orange and lemon juices into the flaming pan of a chafing dish and heat over direct flame until the mixture is hot.

2. Add the sugar, stirring until dissolved.

3. Put a little rum and punsch in a long-handled ladle and warm it by partially submerging the bowl of the ladle in the wine mixture.

4. Ignite and pour the still flaming spirits into the chafing dish.

5. Extinguish flames after a few seconds by covering the pan with its lid.

6. Add the remainder of the rum and punsch. Makes 24 servings.

**STATS**

| SERVE IN | TECHNIQUE | POTENCY | SKILL LEVEL | DANGER |
|----------|-----------|---------|-------------|--------|

# HOT AFRICAN PUNCH

This punch boasts ample booze to raise your spirits, strong black coffee to keep you alert, and enough sugar to rot your teeth! It's a festive once-a-year kind of treat though, so we say indulge with abandon!

Two 750 ml bottles dark Jamaican rum
Four 750 ml bottles brandy

1 gallon hot strong black coffee
4 pounds sugar, preferably superfine

1. Place the sugar in a large pan.

2. Pour the brandy and dark rum over the sugar, turn the heat to medium.

3. Stir the mixture until the sugar dissolves.

4. Ignite the liquid with a long match.

5. Stir with a long metal spoon until the flames are extinguished.

6. Add the coffee and serve hot.

STATS — SERVE IN — TECHNIQUE — POTENCY — SKILL LEVEL — DANGER

# OUT ON THE TOWN...

## FLAMING CHRISTMAS PUNCH

### (COURTESY OF JOSEY PACKARD, BARTENDER AT DRINK IN BOSTON, MA)

You can entertain family and friends with your flame-throwing abilities when preparing this one. Do make sure that your punch bowl is heatproof before you start! Also be sure to extinguish the flames quickly, as otherwise you'll burn away all the alcohol. Use a lid from a pan of similar size, or make one out of heavy-duty aluminum foil.

Josey was inspired to create this masterpiece by a recipe that appeared in the venerable *Esquire's Handbook for Hosts* published in 1949 (a fantastic guide for today's cocktail enthusiast, too). To watch her prepare this punch, check out her December 23, 2009 appearance on the "Cocktail Hour" of the *Rachel Maddow Show* at www.msnbc.com. (Please note: You never know how long these links will remain active, but we decided to risk including this because Josey's instructional demonstration is sure to inspire you!) Check out the way she throws cinnamon and other spices on to the flaming punch to create sparks. Also note, she had three members of the FDNY standing by (and you won't!), so be careful recreating this magical holiday punch at home.

Incidentally, Christmas Punch is not on the menu at Drink. But Josey knows her stuff, so if you're in Beantown, do check out Drink and let Josey make you a delightful cocktail.

Drink • 346 Congress Street • Boston, Massachusetts 02210 • 617-695-1806

| THE BASE: | DILUTING INGREDIENTS: | SPICES FOR THE PYROTECHNICS: | KEEP ON HAND TO EXTINGUISH THE FLAMES: |
|---|---|---|---|
| 3 oranges | Juice of 3 oranges | Ground cinnamon | Pint of apple cider |
| Whole cloves | Juice of 2 lemons | Ground allspice | Pint of water |
| 1 pint dark rum | 1 pint apple cider | Ground nutmeg | |
| 1 pint brandy | 1 pint water | | |
| | ¼ cup sugar | | |

## THE PREP:

Stud the three oranges with the cloves. Roast them for 20 to 30 minutes at 350°F, until softened. Combine the rum and brandy in a heatproof container. Warm the alcohol by immersing the container in hot water. Set the spices for the pyrotechnics aside in small individual cups. Warm the diluting ingredients and have the sugar on hand.

## MAKE THE PUNCH:

Preheat a heatproof punch bowl with hot water from the tap. Put the roasted oranges in the hot, newly emptied bowl. Pour the heated alcohol mixture over the oranges. Ignite the alcohol with a long match. Be aware at all times of how hot the bowl is by touching the outside of it frequently. Carefully toss pinches of the spices at the flame for some added flavor and sparkle.

## PUT OUT THE FLAMES:

Extinguish the flames by pouring the heated cider/water mix over the punch. If the punch doesn't completely extinguish, pour more cider or water over the mixture.

STATS

SERVE IN

TECHNIQUE

POTENCY

SKILL LEVEL

DANGER

# PICCADILLY PUNCH

You don't have to visit London's West End to sample this cinnamon- and clove-spiced concoction, presumably named after Piccadilly Street, a bustling shopping destination built in 1819. But you can relish how the name Piccadilly Punch rolls of your tongue as you serve this robust and warming punch to your guests. The ruby port is optional but delicious.

2 large lemons
12 whole cloves
2 cinnamon sticks
¼ teaspoon nutmeg
1 cup superfine sugar
2 cups hot water or ruby port
One 750 ml bottle cognac

1. Remove the peel from the lemons, stud the peels with cloves, and place in the flaming pan of a chafing dish along with the lemon juice.

2. Add the cinnamon sticks, nutmeg, sugar, and hot water, and simmer, stirring frequently, until all the sugar is dissolved.

3. Warm some cognac in a long-handled ladle.

4. Ignite it, and pour the still blazing cognac into the chafing dish.

5. Extinguish by covering the pan with its lid.

6. Pour the remainder of the cognac into the pan.

7. Stir again and serve hot. Makes about 11 servings.

STATS — SERVE IN   TECHNIQUE   POTENCY   SKILL LEVEL   DANGER

# EAST OF SUEZ

Arak (or arrack, depending on which country is producing it) is a liquor made with fermented fruit, grain, and sugarcane. Arrack, which is found in South and Southeast Asia, typically has a golden amber color, which distinguishes it from the colorless and transparent Middle Eastern arak. This flavorful punch recipe contains the "rum of Indonesia" (aka Batavia arak), a flavor enhancer and powerful spirit. Enjoy this blazing punch with an outrageous Southeast-Asian feast!

| | |
|---|---|
| 1 quart hot black tea | ½ pint Batavia arak |
| 1 lemon, thinly sliced | ½ pint triple sec or curaçao |
| 2 ounces lime juice | 1 pint dark Jamaican rum |
| 1 cup superfine sugar | 1 pint cognac |

1. Combine the tea, lemon slices, lime juice, and sugar into the flaming pan of a chafing dish.

2. Simmer over direct heat until all the sugar is dissolved.

3. Add the arak, triple sec, and rum; heat but don't boil.

4. Warm some cognac in a long-handled ladle by partially submerging the bowl of the ladle in the hot punch.

5. Ignite the cognac and *very carefully* pour it, still blazing, into the chafing dish.

6. After a few seconds, cover the pan with its lid to extinguish the flames.

7. Pour in the remainder of the cognac. Makes about 20 servings.

STATS    SERVE IN    TECHNIQUE    POTENCY    SKILL LEVEL    DANGER

# INDEX

# THANKS!

John Whalen, founder of Cider Mill Press, is the hotshot who came up with the clever idea to create an entire book about flaming shots. Our sincere thanks to him for inviting us to research and write it. Thanks also to Carlo DeVito, another publishing hotshot and owner of the Hudson-Chatham Winery, for introducing us to John. And, finally, our thanks to one more hotshot: our sure-handed project editor Joe Rhatigan, who worked with the talented photographer Steve Mann (www.blackboxphoto.info) and stylish designer Melissa Gerber to turn our manuscript and collection of shot glasses into this eye-catching book.

We also want to thank Drew Wallace of The Admiral in Asheville, North Carolina who was our expert bartender and model. Check out his fine establishment at www.theadmiralnc.com.

Our special thanks go out to Josey Packard (Drink, Boston, MA), Chuck Cerankosky (Good Luck, Rochester, NY), Ales Olasz (Montgomery Place, Notting Hill, London), and Matthew Bax and Matthew Rees (Der Raum, Melbourne, Australia) for being excellent at their craft and for sharing their stories, recipes, and techniques with us.

Finally, hats off to two of New York City's bravest: Chief Mike Casey of Ladder 1, who also happens to own the bar, Red Sky, and Kevin Wrafter, an eleven-year veteran of Engine 6. They provided the fire-safety tips and words of wisdom to ensure that flaming drinks is a fun activity you can enjoy with your friends—and not an occasion for calling 911!

# ABOUT THE
AUTHORS

arah Scheffel is a cookbook editor and writer who divides her time between
rooklyn and Woodstock, New York. She hopes you'll have fun with these flaming
rinks. She also hopes you will not be a flaming idiot.

Christine Gaze is a smart aleck and food and wine enthusiast who lives in New
rk City. She was roped into this project while taking a hiatus from the genteel
orld of finance. She is delighted to have co-authored this book without entering a
2-step program or succumbing to the drink. She hopes you enjoy lighting cocktails
n fire as much as she does.

# ABOUT
# CIDER MILL PRESS

Good ideas ripen with time. From seed to harvest, Cider Mill Press brings fine reading, information, and entertainment together between the covers of its creatively crafted books. Our Cider Mill bears fruit twice a year, publishing a new crop of titles each spring and fall.

**CIDER MILL**
**PRESS**

**BOOK**
**PUBLISHERS**

Visit us on the Web at
www.cidermillpress.com
or write to us at
12 Port Farm Road
Kennebunkport, Maine 04046